10

THINGS

for teen girls

10 THINGS
for teen girls

KATE CONNER

Nashville, Tennessee

978-1-4336-8291-9

Published by B&H Publishing Group

Nashville, Tennessee

Dewey Decimal Classification: 305.23

Subject Heading: GIRLS \ TEENAGERS \ CHRISTIAN LIFE

1 2 3 4 5 6 7   18 17 16 15 14

To all of the dear, beautiful, interesting, incredible teenage girls I've had the privilege to know. I love you. You are enough.

And for Madeline, my sparkle. I love you every single second.

ACKNOWLEDGMENTS

David, Sarah, Dan, and Jana: A million thank yous for reading a million e-mails, editing a million drafts, and answering a million questions. So I guess three million thank yous. You are so, so good at what you do. You made everything better. I am blessed to be on your team.

My friends and family, whose names could fill another book. I am humbled by your friendship. You support, encourage, babysit, laugh, weep, and carry. You are my people. Without you there would be no book.

Jesus, You make me enough. Apart from You I have no good thing. All of this and all of me is from You, and through You, and to You.

TABLE OF CONTENTS

CHAPTER
1

NEON PURPLE LEGGINGS

"Style is a way to say who you are without having to speak." –Rachel Zoe

"Some people think luxury is the opposite of poverty. It is not. It is the opposite of vulgarity." –Coco Chanel

Listen, I know: when adults start to talk about "modesty" you get bored—immediately. It's not your fault. There is an involuntary biochemical reaction bred directly into your brain. It doesn't matter how much you love said adults, or how hard you try to be respectful; it doesn't even matter if you're a super-modest girl—before you even know what's happening, your eyes glaze over and your brain is all, "Here we go again," because you've heard it all before.

I know because it still happens to me. Modesty is a buzzword; I react when I hear it. Usually:

• My eyes glaze over. (And, since it is generally frowned upon for adults to roll their eyes, I open mine really wide to force-quit my eye-roll mechanism. So just know that if I'm ever looking at you with my eyes bugged out like a fruit fly, it's because I'm trying not to roll my eyes at you.)

• I tune out. Daydream. See how long I can hold my breath without anybody noticing, etc.

• I picture white Fruit of the Loom T-shirts under tank tops, the "fingertip" shorts rule, dresses with sleeves—and shoulder pads, bathing suits with skirts attached, and mom jeans.

Another buzzword is "midriff." What is a midriff anyway? Is it different from a stomach? I don't completely understand why it needs its own

word—unless it's to give us clues as to who is speaking. Greater than sixty years old = midriff. Less than sixty years old = stomach.

Talking about modesty feels like a minefield sometimes. There are so many buzzwords that have been twisted and bent and shoved into things they don't really mean. Modesty conversations are like that party game, Taboo—the one in which you have to describe an apple without using the words "computer," "iPod," "fruit," "red," "Mac," "pie," or "Snow White." If you say "modesty," "midriff," "suggestive," "cleavage," "unladylike," or "the fingertip-rule," everyone stops listening: you're out.

But *modesty* is not a dirty Christian word. It's not oppressive or archaic, and I bet you aren't nearly as opposed to the concept of modesty as you are to the word itself.

Sometimes, in the name of real communication, you have to begin by wading through all of the assumptions and preconceived notions, debunking and disarming as you go, before you can start talking about the stuff that matters.

The way we dress is one such opinion-laden, assumption-laden issue.

There are three realities that you need to understand before I will grab you by the proverbial (or literal) shoulders and shake some sense into you about the shorts crawling up your hindquarters and the fact that you HAVE TO WEAR BRAS.

1. Women's bodies are beautiful. (Thank God, glory, hallelujah, amen.)

2. Men like to look at women.

3. That's not bad.

THREE REALITIES

Women's bodies are beautiful.

Boys like breasts. As it turns out, they also like other various girl body parts including, but not limited to: stomachs, lips, hair, necks, thighs, calves, feet, hips, backs, shoulders, elbows, ear lobes, and pinky toes.

Boys aren't weird or obsessive, they're just smart. Girls' bodies are beautiful. One of the great perks of womanhood is that we get to be curvy and soft and inviting. Guys are angular, muscular. And while that's nice enough, they're also hairy.

Femininity is a superpower.

Biologically speaking, adolescence is the time when your superpower emerges. Inconveniently enough, adolescence also places you, a newly-christened superhero of a girl, smack in the middle of the wondrous teenage phase of self-discovery. That's not kitsch—it really is wondrous.

My teenage experience was completely, totally, over-the-moon magical. When I was fifteen I learned that I was good at writing. When I was sixteen I learned that I liked it. When I was thirteen I traveled to France. I studied the language for eight more years and returned after my college graduation, because the language and culture never left me. I rocked high school, with only a handful of hiccups here and there. (Like the time a boy asked me to the

> Femininity is a superpower.

homecoming dance and I didn't want to say "no," so I pretended I didn't hear him and just kept walking onto the bus. That was lame. And mean.) I discovered my sense of humor (funny: hyperbole, puns, wit. Not funny: any joke involving a bodily function). I learned what kind of music I liked; I discovered my spiritual gifts; I overcame chronic, compulsive shyness; I spoke out about my faith; I fell in *actual* love (not with the homecoming/ bus boy, obviously).

This kind of self-discovery and self-expression is intoxicating— addicting! It made me crave more experiences: more concerts, more travel, more movie nights, more cookouts, more surprise parties. More days on the lake, more time with my friends, more hobbies, more road trips. I wanted more and more freedom, not to rebel, but to experience. Self-discovery is deliriously freeing.

Too often, we think modesty is about hiding, which makes sense when all you seem to hear is,

> "Cover that up."

> "No one wants to see that."

> "People will get the wrong idea about you."

"That looks trashy."

"You will not leave this house wearing *that*."

The first thing that you need to understand about modesty is that it's not about hiding or conformity or oppressing women. Hips and breasts are not shameful body parts to be covered up or embarrassed about. Hips and breasts (no matter how big or small) are secret weapons of awesomeness, and it's okay to love them.

Men like to look at women.

Men like to look at women. Even married men. Even *happily* married men. Even good, kind, respectful, stand-up men. Even Christian men. Men are hardwired to enjoy women.

Says who?

Says God. Says the history of mankind, the animal kingdom, natural selection, the Bible, your pastor, and every teenage boy you'll ever meet. The fact that men are hardwired to enjoy women is a fact that pretty much everyone can agree on.

Women are beautiful and men like to look at them. The sooner you accept this, the sooner you'll stop using ridiculous non sequiturs like, "It's not my *fault* I have breasts" to justify buying a prom dress WITHOUT A TORSO. (You're right, it's not your fault you have breasts, but some pieces of clothing shouldn't come in two pieces, and prom dresses are one of them. Are you going tanning at prom? Swimming? Jazzercising?)

A man's desire to look at your body does not make him disrespectful; it makes him a man. It is just as unfair to say "Every man who gapes at women is a creep," as it is to say "Every woman who has big breasts is easy," or "Every girl who wears makeup is vain." It is categorically untrue.

Too often when adults talk about modesty, they make it about going on the defense—about protecting yourself from predators. If you're smart, it won't take you long to see the absurdity of this. A bright girl knows that a man who intends to stare will stare, regardless of what she is wearing. In the same vein, men who have committed *not* to stare, won't.

The notion that a woman can dress in a way that will prevent men from looking at her just doesn't hold water, not in the real world. Baggy sweatpants are not even a deterrent. This line of reasoning leads to oppressive legalism: "Maybe if I just cover up a little more . . ."

It also leads to spandex miniskirts; "If he's going to look anyway, then I might as well wear this."

Women's bodies are beautiful; modesty is not about hiding.

Guys like to look at girls; modesty is not about making yourself immune to stares.

It's not bad.

The fact that guys are biologically hardwired to enjoy girls' bodies is not bad. It's not primitive or dangerous. A man enjoying a woman's body is not perverted, gross, immature, or offensive.

When you get the idea in your head that guys are pigs because they like girls' bodies, everything gets messed up. That kind of thinking makes hyper-feminists hate men, belittle and emasculate them. It makes hyper-conservatives oppress women—insisting they cover up every single body part that might interest a man, creating shame and frustration, even blaming women for their own harassment. On both ends of the very wide spectrum, when women discuss among themselves how gross men are, everybody loses.

A man looking at your body and enjoying it is good. You *want* a man to look at your body and enjoy it.

If you think you don't, it's because you are only considering half of the equation. You think you don't want guys to stare at you, but that's not true. You just don't want the *wrong* guy to stare at you.

When the right man looks at you (to be clear, the right man is the man you marry), you walk a little taller, feel a little more beautiful. When my husband compliments my appearance, I feel secure in my relationship—secure in myself. A little piece of my soul lights up. "I am beautiful! I am enough!" I don't feel uncomfortable because I'm in control. The day I married him I gave him the privilege of enjoying my superpower. He's here by invitation, and as such, his appreciation of me is welcome—and fun.

Modesty is not about making yourself homely or unattractive. Modesty and fashion are not mutually exclusive; neither are modest and beautiful.

Modesty is not about women having to compensate for the poor behavior of men. It is impossible to make yourself immune to leering, and it's not your job, anyway.

Modesty is not about feeling ashamed of breasts, hips, thighs, or any other beautiful, good, superpower body part.

Modesty is not the quenching of self-expression, the endorsement of conformity, or the oppression of femininity.

It's not hard to see why you might buck wildly at modesty when these are the things that come to mind at the mention of the word. No girl in her right mind would say, "Body issues, frustration, shame, ill-fitting clothes, and unattractiveness? Sign me up today!"

But if those are the things that modesty is not, then what *is* it?

NEON PURPLE LEGGINGS

The way we look matters.

It's warmer and fuzzier to say, "It's what's on the inside that counts," and while that is absolutely true, it's not the whole story. The inside matters when you have to stand before God and answer for your life. The inside matters when you're determining your value and worth. The inside matters when you're looking for lasting beauty.

But the outside matters when you're looking for a job.

There isn't one of us who doesn't judge people by their appearances all the time. You'll notice as you walk down the street that there are no cartoon caption bubbles hovering over people's heads that say things like, "I am wearing grease-stained yoga pants and my hair is matted in three or four places because I have four-month-old triplets, and I have not slept in four days," or "It's not that I don't believe in soap, it's just that I changed my own tire on the side of the road LIKE A BOSS. Please excuse the dirty fingernails."

> the inside matters when you're looking for lasting beauty. But the outside matters when you're looking for a job.

(I'm glad that there is no caption bubble hovering over my head because 98 percent of the time it would say, "I have no excuse," or "Have totally let myself go.")

We don't get CliffsNotes on people; and we don't have time to get to know every person we interact with. You can blame the constraints of time and physics for that. When people make assumptions based strictly on physical appearance, it's not because they are shallow—it's because that is the only information they have to go on. These assumptions aren't

character judgments (at least they shouldn't be) but inferences about a person's interests and style.

This makes the clothes you wear a walking advertisement for yourself. They are the closest thing you have to CliffsNotes or a floating cartoon caption bubble.

Clothing speaks; it can say all sorts of things. It can say:

1. My grandmother dressed me for Sunday school today.

2. I spent too much money on this purse.

3. I just came from working out, so I probably have my life together.

4. I have a high-paying, white-collar job, as evidenced by my shiny shoes and power tie. Envy me!

5. Check my tattered flannel shirt! I wish they'd bring back Grunge.

6. Hey, look at my breasts! Look at my breasts!

7. I only listen to bands that nobody has ever heard of.

8. I am obviously colorblind.

9. I like animal prints more than average people do!

10. I didn't feel like doing laundry this month.

Beneath all the pretense and protest and party lines of "I only dress for me," the truth is that people dress to identify with other people. Most of the time, the clothes you choose are either a reflection of who you are or who you want to be. That's why preps dress like preps, hipsters dress like hipsters, indie-boho-free-spirits dress like indie-boho-free-spirits, and so on.

Because clothing speaks, every person who dares venture outside of his or her own living room must ask themselves, "Is mine telling the truth?"

It is your responsibility to create an accurate image for yourself, not the responsibility of the masses to interpret you correctly using their psychic powers.

it iS your responsibility to create an accurate image For yourseIF, not the responsibility OF the masses to interpret you correctly using their PSYCHIC POWers.

The great thing about clothing speaking is that it can satisfy every drop of your need for self-expression; you can make your clothing say anything you want. I've manipulated my clothing to say all sorts of things.

A few years ago I went shopping in New York City. I must have gotten caught up in the giant posters of fashion-forward women in neon clothing and giant, blown-out hair. In hindsight, the techno music was probably a contributing factor because I came home with a pair of neon purple leggings.

I am a stay-at-home mom. My husband is a pastor. IF I leave the house (a big "if"), it is to go to church with lots of little old ladies. I don't know what I thought I was going to do with neon purple leggings, but they seemed very important at the time. I owned those neon purple leggings for an entire year and never wore them once. I would see them lying there in my sock drawer; I would touch them fondly, my fashion-forward neon purple leggings, then close the drawer and pull on my jeans.

The following year, we moved to Alabama—not exactly fashion-forward neon purple leggings territory. On the very first Sunday we were there, I touched my fashion-forward neon purple leggings thoughtfully. It was first impression time, and in a moment of extraordinary courage I decided, "For all these people know, I am the hippest of young mothers, and I come from a place where people wear neon purple leggings all the time." Then I said, "Let there be style!" and I marched into church in my neon purple leggings where people seriously regretted having hired us to come there.

No, but they did say, "You are so stylish, I could never pull that off."

I used my clothing to make a statement about myself. And now, I can wear anything I please and nobody is ever surprised, because in their minds I will always be "the kind of girl who can wear neon purple leggings."

> modesty is about choosing clothes that intentionally communicate what you want the world to know about you.

Modesty is about dressing on purpose. It is about being mature enough to reckon with some realities: the reality that men like to look at women; the reality that if you display your breasts overtly, men will stare, no matter how great the guys are; and the reality that clothing speaks, and that the way you look matters.

Modesty is about choosing clothes that intentionally communicate what you want the world to know about you; it is an integral part of creating your own, truthful image.

BASIC MARKETING

I mentioned how mutually positive and delightful it is when a husband can enjoy his wife visually. It's totally flattering. When the right man looks at your body, you feel affirmed.

Wrong is the polar opposite of right, so it stands to reason that when the *wrong* man looks at your body, you feel the polar opposite of affirmed; you feel degraded.

When the right man enjoys your feminine superpower, he is there by invitation. You are in control and every action, right down to each stolen glance, is based upon mutual trust and respect. You are a whole person that is loved.

When the wrong man enjoys your body, it is a violation. When a man on the street leers, cat-calls, smirks while nodding his head, whispers to his buddies, or makes a crude gesture, it is reprehensible; he is not invited. His staring makes you feel as naked as he is imagining you to be, and the mixture of anger, embarrassment, and disgust twists and burns in your stomach. And please don't buy this nonsense about men admiring God's creation. I know how it feels to be noticed by men, and I know how it feels to be objectified. There is a discernable difference in both the behavior and in the way it makes me feel. I have to believe that we all know the difference. I refuse to shame the noticing, and, just as vehemently, I refuse to tolerate the objectifying.

Modesty is about taking control. Dressing modestly is a way of telling every man in the world, "I have not given you permission to stare at my breasts. That privilege belongs to a man who knows me—my personality, my handwriting, my family, my stories—my whole self. I am not a Playboy bunny; I do not exist for the entertainment of men. I am more than that, so you don't get to use me that way, even in passing."

Dressing modestly is about harnessing your superpower.

Let me be clear, women who dress provocatively do not deserve to be disrespected, degraded, or violated in any way. Ever. A woman in the buff is still not "asking for it." But if a woman dresses provocatively and does not *relish* the attention her body garners from men, she is not telling the truth with her clothing. There is a breakdown in communication, a disconnect.

This is basic marketing—PR, reputation management. We are all our own agents, and you must represent yourself well. If you don't mind being viewed as a sex object without thoughts, feelings, or skills outside of the bedroom, then by all means, dress to call attention to your sex organs. I can't fault that logic; it is at least consistent. But if you want to be known for your great ideas or your cross-country running accomplishments, you have to put those things in the display case.

If you want to be known for your humor, your kindness, your eyes, your thoughts on social issues, your athleticism, or your confidence, you must put those things on display more prominently than your breasts.

While there is no body part you can accentuate with a good belt to communicate kindness, you can ensure that a man isn't allowed to enjoy your breasts until he's gotten to know *all about* your kindness, among other things.

Listen, your body is beautiful, but you are more than a body. It would be such a shame if you made it so easy for people to ignore the rest of you.

Modesty allows people to see the rest of you—to see the best of you.

> modesty allows people to see the rest of you—to see the best of you.

ON ATTRACTING MEN

I work with teenage girls every single day. I don't have enough fingers and toes to count how many times one of you has come to me, baffled and disillusioned, plopped down on my couch and said with a huff, *"I only attract jerks."*[1]

My response is always the same: "Every woman attracts a handful of creeps in her lifetime. You're not broken; it just means you're a beautiful girl. But (sorry, there is a "but") if you are *only* attracting creeps, there might be something to discuss."

Then I drop the bomb.

"If the guys who want to date you:

- leave as soon as they get what they want

- don't make any effort to get to know what you're thinking and feeling

- constantly try to put their hands on your body

- seem too interested in the bodies of other girls[2]

---

1. "Jerks can be substituted with "creeps," or "idiots," and other more colorful terms.
2. Use this list as a litmus test; if these four behaviors describe the boy you're dating, get out. At best, he's incredibly immature and not ready for a relationship. More likely, he has an unhealthy view of girls, which will cause you to be objectified, disrespected, and hurt.

If you notice a long line of losers, you have to ask yourself, *What am I doing that is causing these creeps to flock?"*

This is almost always met with stunned silence as the teenager tries to decide whether or not I've offended her. I forge ahead quickly before I get the involuntary eye-roll and she's gone forever.

"The truth is that, by and large, you'll attract what you bait. Are you carrying yourself to bait godly young men? Or boys that just want you for your body?"

LOOKS OF HORROR. This is the point in the conversation at which the girls start tugging at their tank tops to cover up their cleavage.

We are getting back to the very basics of math here—back to common sense and the most primal laws of attraction.

Guys who value compassion are drawn to compassionate girls. Guys who value intelligence are drawn to intelligent girls. Guys who value style are drawn to stylish girls. Guys who value bacon are drawn to girls who cook bacon. THERE IS A PATTERN HERE.

If you want to date a godly man—a man who wants to marry a godly woman—then you should endeavor to be the godly woman he is seeking.

If your figure outshines your positivity and personality as the most prominent thing about you, then you are baiting the kind of boy whose primary interest is what is under your shirt and how easily he can access it.

Ask yourself who you're baiting, and don't sugarcoat the answer— tell yourself the truth.

The other issue at hand is that when you display your body without much reservation, you are shutting down all the male brains in the vicinity. I was so not kidding when I called it a superpower. You can SHUT DOWN MEN'S BRAINS. Studies show that sex (and related matter) turns off higher brain functions in men; they start thinking with their hormones, if you will. This is precisely why the girls who regularly dress provocatively are the same ones complaining about what mindless brutes men are.

A 2008 Princeton University study,[3] originally published in the *Journal of Cognitive Neuroscience,* revealed that when men viewed images of bikini-clad women, the part of their brains associated with tools and the intention to commit action lit up. There was also a remarkable inactivity in the part of the brain that processes another person's thoughts and feelings. No human interaction and a desire to use and act upon; this is the very definition of objectification. It turns you into an object. A supplementary study revealed that men associated images of women in bikinis with first-person verbs like "I handle. I push. I grab." The same men associated pictures of women dressed in casual business attire with third-person verbs: "She handles. She pushes. She grabs." In one scenario, the women were out of control (being acted upon), and in the other the women were in control (the ones doing the acting). So don't get too excited about the ability to turn a man's brain off—it's not as flattering as you think.

It is so important to note that these findings aren't bad. They don't indicate that men are flawed or innately disrespectful. They simply reveal information about the (God-created and "very good"[4]) male brain. The takeaway is that if we, as women, want to be viewed as whole people, we must present ourselves as whole people. The logical conclusion is that, because there appears to be some hardwiring that makes it difficult for men to engage

> iF We Want to Be VieWeD aS WHOle PeOPle, We muSt PreSent OurSelveS aS WHOle PeOPle.

---

3. See http://www.mitpressjournals.org/doi/abs/10.1162/jocn.2010.21497.
4. God's words, not mine.

a sexily-dressed woman on a deeper level, we should dress in a way that allows us to be taken seriously.

Here's one reason this matters: If you want a meaningful relationship—if you want a guy to value qualities in you besides your cup size (spoiler alert: you do)—you're going to need his higher brain function intact. In other words, put on some more clothes so that you can engage the opposite sex on a higher brain wave. Everybody wins.

THE CRUX OF THE MATTER: THE HEART

I fear that up until this point, I may have oversimplified the matter. Everything I've written is practical, tried, and true, but it's also operating on a dangerous assumption.

It is operating on the assumption that smart, bright young women do not wish to be thought of as sex objects. But the sticky thing is, some do. Some of you have been seduced by the power of it. You relish the ability to turn a man's brain to mush. You delight in wielding your superpower over the first boy who comes close enough to be manipulated—you're flattered by the knowledge that you can flash a little skin and get anything you want. No amount of science or common sense can talk you out of immodesty if immodesty is your goal.

This is a sin-sick heart problem, and it cannot be remedied by logic.

When C. S. Lewis reflected on our sin-sick heart problems, he wrote, "It would seem that Our Lord finds our desires not too strong, but too weak. . . . We are far too easily pleased."

This is simply, exactly, correct. The part of your heart that seeks to be found beautiful has been twisted and perverted into a desperate desire for attention. It's not that you desire attention too much; it is that you don't desire what is greater: respect.

All attention is not equal. It is possible to get a man's attention and *never* have his respect.

You can't revel in the attention your breasts elicit from men, and then be offended that your breasts are all they're interested in. You wanted attention, and you got it.

You can't delight in men's drooling, be flattered by their stammering, manipulate them with your miniskirt, and then be surprised when your body is the only thing they care about. You wanted attention, and you got it.

You should never settle for the ability to make a man drool when you could have his admiration.

Sweet sisters, all attention is not equal. You think you want attention, but you don't. You want respect.

Use modesty as a tool to pursue that which is greater: admiration, respect, and love.

> all attention is not equal..
> you think you want
> attention, but you don't.
> you want respect.

THINK IT THROUGH, TALK IT OUT

1. What comes to mind when you think about modesty?

2. Modest really just means "not drawing attention to yourself." It has absolutely nothing to do with sex or lust or provocation. (Revealing clothes are just a surefire way to draw attention to yourself, which is why people spend so much time talking about them.) Why do you think God tells people (guys and girls) to dress modestly?

3. If you had a floating CliffsNotes bubble over your head that summed up your daily life in a sentence or two, what would it say?

4. Who do you dress for? School authorities? A sports team? Parents? Friends? The cool kids? A boy? An employer or interviewer? Do you think it's okay to dress for other people, or should you only dress for yourself?

5. Think about your favorite outfit and the two or three outfits that you wear the most often: what do those clothes tell the world about you?

6. If you could have your appearance say *anything*, what would you want it to communicate?

7. What are small, doable steps you can take to make that a reality? Are there clothing pieces that you need to invest in? Pieces you need to give away? An attitude shift? How can you change the way you take care of your clothing/appearance?

8. What is the difference between attention and respect?

9. Why do girls settle for attention? Think for a moment: have you settled for attention?

10. What things can you and your friends do to insist on respect?

CHAPTER

2

THE TANNING B̶E̶D̶ TRAP

> *"In 1,000 years, archaeologists will find tanning beds and think that we fried people as punishment." -Tumblr*

I am not just Irish; I am super-Irish.

My name is Kathryn Elizabeth. I have freckles and auburn hair. My grandparents lived in Dublin for thirty years; my mother went to high school there; and I had visited by the time I was three. I have tea almost every day; I love potatoes and U2; I grew up listening to Makem and Clancy and watching a Riverdance VHS tape. I know all the words to "Danny Boy," "The Fox", "Wild Rover," "Mary Mack," "When Irish Eyes Are Smiling," and "All God's Creatures Got a Place in the Choir."

Do you know what this means? This means that I will never have a tan as long as I live.

This means that as a child, while all my friends were plunging their bronzed bikini-ed bodies into the ocean, I was getting slathered with SPF 50—under my T-shirt.

This means that my cheeks are ruddy seven days a week, and that when I get hot, they turn so bright and blotchy it looks like somebody crushed slices of ripe watermelon on them.

WHEN i WaS in tHE SiXtH GraDE i StarteD HatinG mY SKin—anD Felt SHame aBout it For tHE next nine years.

It means that when I was in the eighth grade and decided to lighten my hair with lemon juice and peroxide,[5] it turned bright, brassy orange, and my cheeks were ruddy with embarrassment for months.

---

5. NEVER, EVER, EVER DO THIS, even under threat of violence. That tidbit is free, you're welcome.

It means that my skin is so fair that you can see my hair straight through it. It means that I could shave three times today and still have a million dark speckles up and down my legs from hairs that will grow tomorrow.

It means that in the winter months I cannot find makeup light enough. "Porcelain Ivory," which is the fairest shade available at the drugstore, is too dark. (A friend once suggested Wite-Out, and I will be trying it this winter. I'll keep you posted.)

It means that when I was in the sixth grade I started hating my skin—and felt shame about it for the next nine years.

I was in the eleventh grade the first time I set foot into a tanning bed. (This was after several self-tanning creams gone awry—and by awry, I mean orange, streaky, and more than a little conspicuous around the ankles.)

The experience was a pale girl's worst nightmare (besides, of course, staying pale forever). The salon was manned by a petite lady with skin the color of a burnt sienna Crayola crayon, and the whole place smelled like a coconut stuffed inside a sweaty sock. There was an intimidating case full of lotions up front: accelerators, calming creams, and mystery products in opaque bottles plastered with pictures of neon parrots.

The lady asked me if I'd ever been tanning before, and when I said no, I had to sign a waiver.

Note: Any activity that requires you to sign a waiver PROBABLY ISN'T THE SAFEST.

After I agreed not to sue her extended family if I got skin cancer, the lady asked me how long I'd like to tan. I was unprepared for this question. I stared at her blankly.

"Most people go in for eleven or twelve minutes the first time," she offered after an uncomfortable silence.

"Maybe six then," I whispered.

She rolled her eyes and pulled a pair of goggles out of a canister of blue juice—the same, supposedly sanitary, blue juice that the combs sit in at the hair salon. She told me that the bed would turn on automatically in two minutes.

Two minutes?!

I galloped awkwardly down the hall, strapping the moist goggles to my head as I went—I didn't want to get cancer *and* be blind. The goggles were so tight that they suctioned themselves to my eye sockets with a loud *schlooop*! Everything went black and began to spin. Here I faced a critical decision: keep the goggles on and fumble around in the blackness trying to undress myself? Or take off the goggles, undress, and hopefully replace them before the ultraviolet rays burned out my retinas?

And speaking of undressing—what degree of undress is appropriate in this situation? I didn't bring a bathing suit—that seemed like a rookie mistake. And though I was SO OBVIOUSLY a tanning novice, I was determined not to look like one. **Spoiler alert: too late.**

I decided to take off the goggles.

Once the blood started flowing back into my brain, I noticed a small pile of towels and a spray bottle full of more blue juice. I deduced that this was for sanitizing the bed. Here I faced a second critical decision: sanitize the bed before putting the goggles on—was there time for this? Or lay my delicate, bare, Irish skin onto a surface where another person's skin had previously lain—sweating? Or put the goggles on first, and try to stay upright long enough to sanitize the bed, which would likely result in my passing out on the ground, naked, with one arm in the tanning bed holding a spray bottle and badly burned.

I sensed that my two minutes were almost up; the pressure was mounting. I was still fully clothed, holding the spray bottle in one hand and the death goggles in the other. Time was running out! I felt like I was on a bomb squad; and I had thirty seconds to diffuse a bomb before detonation. I panicked. I whipped off my shirt, clenched my eyes shut, and started spritzing furiously. I spiked the bottle, grabbed a towel, and swiped at the bed blindly, mopping off what I could while trying to unbutton my jeans.

You guys, I'm such a professional. Somebody's got to keep it classy, might as well be me.

I decided to leave my undergarments on, mostly because I was in too desperate a state to consider the alternative; I did not have the mental energy to make that kind of decision. I suctioned the goggles back to my head and slid my leg onto the bed just as the lights buzzed to life. Close call.

Then my elbow found a puddle of unmopped juice and I landed clumsily into full tanning position with an ungraceful thud.

Okay, so far so good.

Another thing nobody thought to mention is that there is a time-space continuum thing happening inside of tanning beds. You know how God says that a thousand years are like a day to Him and a day is like a thousand years? I think God was in a tanning bed when He said that, because one tanning-bed-minute feels like *at least* one thousand real-life minutes. A six-minute stay in a tanning bed feels like an eternity lost in the Sahara.

I didn't breathe for the first minute, which felt like an hour.

During the second minute I exhaled.

During the third minute I peeped my eyes open. The skin around them was so puffed up from the goggles that I couldn't see properly. Everything looked distorted—blue and ethereal. I thought, *Lord, this must be what it looks like when people get abducted by aliens.*[6]

During the fourth minute I thought, *It's actually quite nice in here— warm, relaxing. Ahhhhhh. I'm going to look like a Greek goddess when I get out of this thing, which should be any minute now.*

During the fifth minute I thought, *It has definitely been longer than six minutes. Sweet merciful heavens, she forgot about me. I don't know where the off-switch is! And I can't find it with these blasted goggles on my face! Oh Jesus. Jesus, I love You; please turn it off, please turn it off, please turn it off, please turn it off.*

During the sixth minute I thought, *I AM GOING TO DIE IN HERE! How is it legal for something to get this hot? I am dehydrated! I am burned! My skin! My retinas! HELP!!! And for the love of all the kittens, WHAT IS WRONG WITH THESE GOGGLES!?!?!*

Then the tanning bed clicked off.

I climbed out, stunned, sweaty, and cheeks ruddier than they had ever been. I sanitized the bed as a courtesy, put my clothes back on, and left—smelling a little like a coconut stuffed inside a sweaty sock.

You would think that after such a traumatic inaugural experience that my first trip to the tanning bed would have been my last. I'm sorry to say that it was not.

I tanned only very occasionally through high school: a week before each dance and one before summer. I took it easy mostly because my mom took to leaving pamphlets about melanomas on my pillow. So subtle. The first time she did it, I walked into my bedroom, picked up

---

6. I do not really believe in aliens.

the brochure, and curled my lip in disgust when I saw the rotted-looking black spots on an old man's arm.

"What *IS* this?" I asked her.

"Oh, I just saw it at work and thought it was interesting. Did you know that sun damage is cumulative? That even though a burn goes away the damage never does? That every sunburn you get builds on the one before it? Did you know that one bad burn can do irreparable damage to your skin? DID YOU????"

"Uh . . . no. But now I do. Thanks, Mom. Do you, uh, want these pictures back?"

"No, you can keep them," she chirped.

"Whatever."

"I don't tan often," I reasoned to myself every time I went. "And I don't use any weird lotions or lay out for hours."

If you tan, chances are you say those things too. You might even have excuses that weren't available to me, like, "I never burn. I don't need sunscreen. I have naturally tan skin. My grandparents were (fill in the blank with some sun-tolerant ethnicity)." You also probably insist that it clears up your skin (okay, that's true) and that it will keep you from getting burned during your first pool trips of the summer.[7] Blah, blah, blah.

My most habitual tanning happened during my freshmen year of college. That year, my friend Nicole discovered Kitty's. "Kitty's Hair and Tanning" was a dingy building in a gravel parking lot, twelve miles from campus. That we willingly set foot into that place is our everlasting shame.

---

7. You know what else does this? Sunscreen.

Kitty was a leathery woman dressed in pink with an impressive Jeri curl perched on top of her head.

Kitty had four tanning beds in the back of her one-room salon ("salon" is a generous word), presumably from the eighties, just like the curling, yellowed posters on the walls. Kitty charged two dollars per session. Two bucks!

Nicole and I were broke college students with no mothers to leave melanoma pamphlets on our pillows—and we were sold. For three months I tanned recreationally—at least three times a week. I grew accustomed to the tanning ritual (I even learned how to work the goggles), and the more my tanning-savvy grew, the more I was convinced that no trip to the tanning bed would ever be as traumatic as my first.

I was wrong.

One day, Nicole and I headed to Kitty's after class for an afternoon tanning session. We pulled off the rural highway to find the gravel parking lot deserted. We walked to the door and were surprised to find it cracked. We stuck our noses inside to find an old man inside sweeping up hair; he looked like he could have been homeless. When he saw us craning our necks through the crack in the door, he told us that Kitty had left early and that he was just locking up.

Now, if you want proof that tanning kills brain cells, here it is: when this strange, homeless-looking man offered to let us tan, alone in the building, after hours, we said *yes*.

It was not until I was scantily clad and trapped inside a giant glowing bed that I thought, *Who was that guy? I've never seen him around before. He could lock the doors! He could be coming in here right now! He could be walking in on Nicole right now! Nobody will ever hear us scream!*

I held my breath, listening, and looking for anything with which I could inflict physical harm. I decided that the big fan standing in the corner was my best shot. Blunt force trauma. When my bed clicked off, I dressed hurriedly, grabbed my keys (shoved between my fingers, poised to jab eyeballs), and Nic and I booked it out of there.

On the way home, Nicole told me that while I was thinking about how to rescue her, she was thinking about how to rescue me. She told me that her weapon of choice would have been the curling irons that stay heated up in their little holders (so much better than my fan-plan). That is friendship. When you find a friend willing to run naked out of a tanning bed and stab an old man with a hot curling iron for you—you keep her.

After two semesters' worth of textbooks, pizza, and ill-advised trips to Kitty's, I was flat broke. Tanning lost some of its allure—due mostly to my extreme poverty and crippling guilt.

Providentially, it was at precisely this time that God introduced me to Leslie—a woman to whom I am forever indebted. It was Leslie who taught me about The Beauty Trap.

THE BEAUTY TRAP

I was sitting on a cold, tile floor with seventy other girls from my dorm when everything I ever thought about my skin (and my weight) changed forever.

Leslie, the woman who would become my mentor for the remainder of the semester, said, "I've heard a thousand and one self-esteem messages in my life, and none of them has had much impact on my self-esteem. That's why this is not a self-esteem message. I want to show you how I know that beauty is a trap."

Then, together, we looked through the annals of history.

During the Middle Ages, the masses labored outdoors all day, just to survive. They worked to grow food, collect water, and maintain the land of their feudal lords. Women labored strenuously and had precious little food; they were thin. Women worked outdoors as long as it was daylight; they were dark. And when you flip through a textbook or stroll through an art museum you'll notice: the standard for beauty during the Middle Ages was a thick—even overweight—woman; the fairer the better. It represented wealth. The most elusive body type, the one nearly impossible to attain under the circumstances of the day, was beautiful.

In stark contrast to the Middle Ages stands America today. The American masses work sedentary jobs, all indoors. We work in offices and cubicles, virtually chained to computer monitors all day long. We leave for work before the sun is up and return after it's set. Our food-cooking, clothes-washing machines (for which I'm very grateful) make hard physical labor all but obsolete. We have an abundance of food—of cheap, convenient unhealthy food. On any given night we can choose: Mexican? Chinese? Thai? Indian? Italian? American? Moroccan? We live in a technologically dependent, drive-through world. And when you turn on the television, behold! Our standard for beauty is a disproportionately thin woman; the tanner the better. The most elusive body type, nearly impossible to attain under the circumstances of the day, is beautiful.

It was the same in every culture, in every era. I couldn't believe it.

> i could hear the collective yearning of every woman in history who ever spent her life chasing after an ideal that was a setup from the start.

It was like my whole life I'd been looking at the issue of "beauty" through a peephole. I knew that the industry *today* was a trap; I knew that women with straight hair wanted curly hair and women with curly hair wanted straight hair. I knew that shapely girls wanted to be thin and that thin girls wanted breasts so badly they could die. But as

Leslie walked us through history that night, it was like someone swung the whole door wide open. Suddenly, I wasn't just looking at *my* body, *my* skin, *my* self-esteem; suddenly I could hear the collective yearning of every woman in history who ever spent her life chasing after an ideal that was a setup from the start.

Suddenly, I was mad.

This trap—this cruel, sadistic trap—is why fair, freckled girls give themselves sun poisoning and blisters and cancer to be tan, and think they're getting a good deal. This evil trap is why dark girls bleach their skin trying to pass the "brown paper bag test" and assume that it just comes with the territory. It's why half of the cosmetic surgeries out there are to make women thinner and the other half are to put a little more junk into women's proverbial trunks.

It's ludicrous! It's senseless that we can find beauty in literally every type of girl but can't for the life of us find it in ourselves.

And Satan laughs at our dissatisfaction. He smacks his lips, laps it up, and revels in it. I hate him. I hate Satan for causing pain, but even more for enjoying it. If I'm not careful, I sometimes find myself thinking that Satan is just doing his job, fulfilling his cosmic role. I imagine him as an actor cast to play the villain—just an archetype. But he IS the villain. He connives to orchestrate our destruction; he mocks our inner aching, our jealousy, and our self-harm. I hate him.

> it's ludicrous! it's senseless that we can find Beauty in literally every type of Girl But can't for the life of us find it in ourselves.

I refuse to be a victim of the beauty trap; you will not find me among its casualties.

I refuse to tan because, why should I have to be tan? Because I want to? This begs the question why I want to. Because it's beautiful? Well, so is fair. I reject the notion that whatever I am not is more beautiful than what I am. I refuse to dwell in perpetual striving and maddening insecurity.

I believe in health. I believe in caring for my body well. I will not ignore weight that I should lose under the pretense of embracing self-esteem. I believe in exercise, good food choices, and hygiene. I believe in fashion, style, and makeup. I believe in making the most of what I've got. But I think that as a human race we've got it all wrong. I believe God thought up beauty and splashed it all over creation and humankind for us to enjoy. I believe it's not nearly as narrow or elusive as we've been conditioned to believe. And above all else, I believe that

> i reject the notion that whatever i am not is more Beautiful than what i am.

as the creator of beauty, God must know the truth about it. I rest in the fact that what He tells me about beauty is not a snare, but a healing balm.

The king is enthralled by your beauty; honor him, for he is your lord." (Psalm 45:11)

All beautiful you are, my darling; there is no flaw in you. (Song of Solomon 4:7)

For you created my inmost being; you knit me together in my mother's womb. I praise you because I am fearfully and wonderfully made; your works are wonderful, I know that full well. My frame was not hidden from you when I was made in the secret place. When I was woven together in the depths of the earth, your eyes saw my unformed body. All the days ordained for me were written in your book before one of them came to be. (Psalm 139:13–16)

"The LORD does not look at the things man looks at. Man looks at the outward appearance, but the LORD looks at the heart." (1 Samuel 16:7)

Charm is deceptive, and beauty is fleeting; but a woman who fears the LORD is to be praised. (Proverbs 31:30)

The perfect shade of skin for you is the one you have. The perfect body frame is the one you've got. Real beauty doesn't trap you; it frees you. Real beauty doesn't make you die inside; it makes you come alive.

THINK IT THROUGH, TALK IT OUT

1. Have you ever been to a tanning bed?

2. What is the most radical thing you've ever done to try to alter your natural appearance?

3. Was the outcome good, bad, or a little bit of both? Explain.

4. The Beauty Trap means that we always admire that which: 1) we don't have, and 2) would be next to impossible for us to achieve. How have you experienced The Beauty Trap personally? Do you see it in play at your school? How have we experienced it as a society?

5. Kate said, "I reject the notion that whatever I am not is more beautiful than what I am." What physical feature do you like about yourself? What feature do you need to make peace with? Maybe even learn to love?

6. Where should your beauty come from, according to 1 Peter 3:3–4? How does this make you feel? Do you think this puts more pressure on us as girls, or less pressure?

CHAPTER
3

IN THE CAFETERIA
WITH A MEGAPHONE

> "If you are not kind on the Internet, then you're not kind." —Glennon Melton[8]

Before 2007, teenage girls were not allowed on Facebook.

It was a simpler time.

If you had been born ten years earlier, you would be as bad at texting as your mom is. You would be as clueless about the Internet as your parents. And you wouldn't have been able to post cryptic song lyrics as your status when your eighth grade boyfriend broke up with you because you RAN[9] AWAY FROM HIM so you wouldn't have to hold his hand or make conversation. What, that never happened to you? Only me? Okay, whatever. The point is, if you'd been born ten years earlier, you wouldn't have had a hundred friends to like your status to show their support; you would have had to lock yourself in your bedroom and listen to a Brandy song on repeat for three days just to cope with your colossal failure as a teenage girl. I'm still speaking hypothetically, of course. You would have had to find a group of friends willing to listen to your melodrama, and chances are they would only want to hear it about eight times. The other 984,708,157 times, you would have been on your own.

If you had been born ten years earlier, and you wanted to win allies in the battle against your parents, you would have had to explain how backwards and unaware they were to each friend individually, instead of posting a quick "INSAAAAAANE!" status. It took much longer to amass forces.

If you wanted to passive-aggressively confront a friend about her behavior, you would have had to get creative about it. Let me drop some

---

8. See http://momastery.com/blog/2013/07/01/momaquery-on-criticism-vs-cruelty.

9. I literally ran from my 6th period class straight onto the school bus. He called me that afternoon—to break up with me. SURPRISE!

experience on you here: the best way to do this was to write a fake note to a *mutual* friend and leave it in a place where the offending friend would find it—and thereby deduce that all her friends were talking about her behind her back.

You would have had to be a lot craftier before 2007.

Today, Facebook offers you the luxury of whining, complaining, arguing, gossiping, attention-seeking, and passive-aggressively attacking anyone who crosses you with the click of a mouse. And it feels *amazing*.

Facebook is a master at getting us to open up, right? It's a real conversational wizard. It asks, caringly, "What's on your mind?"

Prompted by such sincere interest, you'll tell Facebook anything. You tell Facebook things you wouldn't dare tell your parents, your friends, or your hairdresser.

You fill in the box dutifully. Gratefully. Much too honestly.

Then, because you're feeling so empowered and validated, you click "Share!"

Et voilà. Your most private thoughts in black and white before your eyes. It is official. You are heard.

Facebook gives us humans something we've always wanted—something we crave: a captive audience. Facebook always listens.

> FaceBook Gives us Humans sometHing we've always wanted—sometHing we crave: a captive auDience.

Facebook doesn't judge us. Facebook hears where we're coming from. Facebook knows how smart we are. How mature we are. How unappreciated we are. How right we are.

Facebook is a dream come true in that way. The days of venting in front of mirrors, imagining what it would be like to really let someone have it are over. No more writing entire conversations in your head like

> **tHe Great irony is tHat WHat you Write to no one can Be Seen By everyone.**

a movie script, no more imagining how sorry someone would be if they could see you crying in your bedroom. Facebook makes all of this irrelevant. Now you can just *tell everyone* that you are crying in your bedroom.

In 2007, Facebook opened itself up to the general public, allowing you to type up what you were feeling to no one in particular. The great irony is that what you write to no one can be seen by everyone.

And thus, the age of oversharing was born.

ANONYMITY

There is an Internet lie out there making its rounds and sinking its teeth into your brain (and the brains of all the adults too). The lie is this:

"If it's anonymous, it doesn't count."

If nobody knows who I'm talking about, no harm done.

If nobody knows it was I who said it, there can be no consequences.

If I don't name names, it's not gossip.

Each of these is, in a word, *hogwash*. We embrace them to appease our consciences. They are lies we live with to justify our rampant oversharing.

You guys, the Internet is not anonymous. The Internet is not private and THAT'S THE POINT. The Internet's whole job is to connect: to connect you to people and information and resources you wouldn't have any other way. The Internet is like a Broadway stage, and it's really good at what it does: display stuff. There is no such thing as Internet privacy.

And even if the Internet were private, which it's not, it still wouldn't justify the kind of things you share on there. Words are swords. They can be used powerfully for good or evil and they have the ability to cut us to the quick. It doesn't matter if you can't see who's wielding a sword—it cuts you just the same. Anonymous swords can still make you bleed.

> WORDS are SWORDS. They can be used powerfully for good or evil and they have the ability to cut us to the quick.

I cannot count on hands and feet the number of Facebook statuses I've read from teen girls that sound something like this:

"I hate how these girls are all talk and then when you go confront them about it they wanna back down and try to be all innocent when you know the truth."

"You will never know how I feel because I will never tell you. I can't trust you enough to tell you what I feel without you putting me down and hurting me. So I'd rather just feel bad."

"Tired of guys playing games. If you did it then tell me! Don't lie! Because there is NO reason for it. You're just stupid by even doing that. You're a jerk, don't talk to me anymore if you're going to pull that stuff. "

"When you know someone for almost two years and they turn on you and lie to you but they want YOU to tell the truth and you do. I'm done with stuck-up people these days."

"If they wanna talk to me they know how to reach me. I'm done texting people to be ignored."[10]

---

10. These are real Facebook statuses collected from teenagers I know, however loosely, in 2012. I took the liberty of correcting just enough of the grammatical and spelling errors to make them decipherable.

Girls, I love you, and you've got to know: there is nothing more juvenile than an emotional, passive-aggressive accusation directed at someone whose identity is so thinly-veiled that an orangutan could figure it out.

> tHere is notHinG more Juvenile tHan an emotional, Passive—aGGressive accusation DirecteD at someone WHOse iDentitY is so tHinlY—VeileD tHat an oranGutan coulD FiGure it out.

Walk through this with me: the people who can read your Facebook statuses are the people you have added as your Facebook "friends."[11] And do you know who you've added as your "friends"? YOUR FRIENDS. When you post a status update, your friends from school, band, sports teams, church, work, and the neighborhood read it. Therefore, a passive-aggressive Facebook status is essentially the same thing as your mom calling all her mom-friends and saying, "I hate it when *some husbands* leave coffee grounds all over the floor. Come on, you're a grown man."

I mean, that's insane. And petty. And weird. And mean.

I know it doesn't *feel* the same thing as you posting a Facebook status, but that's just because the Internet and everyone on it has very bad manners—and you grew up with the Internet. It's like commonly accepted social rules don't apply on the Internet, even though the people there are still subject to social hurts. It doesn't add up; it's a recipe for disaster. Social media is not its own separate world anymore; it is a

---

11. I am making a very dangerous assumption here that you do not have your privacy settings set to "public." If you do, change it to private, stat. You are not going to get famous or get a husband by leaving your settings on public. Any man trolling FB for girls he doesn't even have mutual friends, which is not the kind of dude you want to date. There are a hundred reasons your privacy settings matter, not the least of which is your safety.

part of real life—an integral part of the way you interact with everyone you know. You've got to understand that posting a Facebook status that references another person accomplishes the same thing as standing up on a table in the cafeteria with a megaphone and announcing,

"I hate it when CERTAIN PEOPLE (cough, cough) don't text me back!"

Ninety percent of the people in the cafeteria would know exactly who you're talking about—the rest are so engrossed in their rectangular cafeteria pizza that the chemistry teacher could streak through the room in nothing but a lab coat and they would just keep plucking off the little pepperoni cubes. You are classmates! Mutual friends. None of them are so dense that they cannot deduce who the offending non-texter-backer is.

Here is what happens when you post a Facebook status like that:

1. It makes you look sullen and pouty.

2. You look immature and self-involved.

3. Those who *know* to whom you are referring make unfair judgments about the non-texter-backer.

4. The non-texter-backer gets mad, hurt, offended, and embarrassed.

5. The non-texter-backer has a reason to hold a grudge or retaliate.

In no real-life situation is this kind of public denouncement of another person acceptable, but the false sense of anonymity granted by Facebook makes it fair game for you. The result is drama on a cosmic scale. But you already know about the drama.

You would do well to remember that you are not a Navaho wind talker; that people are, *shockingly*, capable of cracking your super-duper secret code. Anybody over the age of six can read between the lines—and words, like swords, have no regard for anonymity. Anonymous swords wielded by anonymous foes slice hearts and friendships into broken, bleeding pieces.

So please, make sure to use your Facebook statuses not as instruments of wickedness, but as instruments of grace.

Do not offer the parts of your body to sin, as instruments of wickedness, but rather offer yourselves to God, as those who have been brought from death to life; and offer the parts of your body to him as instruments of righteousness. For sin shall not be your master, because you are not under law, but under grace. (Romans 6:13–14)

Every username, every avatar, Twitter handle, and profile picture is a real person with real feelings. Just because you interact with them through a monitor doesn't remove the imperative to be nice. I love how Glennon Melton said it, "If you are not kind on the Internet, then you are not kind."

> JUST BeCaUSe YOU interact WitH tHem tHroUGH a monitor DoeSn't remove tHe imperative to Be nice.

TECHNOLOGY IS NEUTRAL

While Facebook has certainly upped the ante for drama you can produce in a day, I'm not for deleting Facebook. Facebook is not the problem. Facebook is just the poor scapegoat.

As weary as I am of reading teen Facebook statuses like, "Stop flirting with my man! You know who you are!" I am EQUALLY fed up with hearing parents gripe,

"Facebook is taking away her real-life friends."

"Facebook causes drama."

"Facebook is addictive."

"Twitter is making us narcissistic."

"Twitter is a time-suck."

"Pinterest is making us stupid."

"Pinterest is making us feel jealous and inferior as mothers and housekeepers."

I'm fed up with it because it's not true.

Facebook doesn't cause drama; **people** cause drama.

Facebook doesn't isolate you; **you** isolate you.

Twitter doesn't suck your time; **you** waste your time.

Twitter doesn't make anyone narcissistic; it gives people an outlet for displaying their previously existing narcissism.

I believe that social media (like almost every other thing) is neutral. It isn't innately awesome or innately terrible; it is what you make it.

I can say with a clear conscience that Facebook has never given me a single moment of anxiety. You might not believe me because this sounds so *otherworldly* to you that it blows your mind—but it's true.

The reason that Facebook has never caused a problem for me is that I refrain from posting anything that I wouldn't want every single person on my friends' list to see. If there is one soul—one ex-boyfriend, one stranger—that I wouldn't want to know exactly how I'm feeling or what I did this afternoon, I don't share it publicly; and the Internet is a public place.

So try not to be shocked when Facebook doesn't treat your deepest secrets delicately. The News Feeds of the masses aren't a diary or a trusted friend; they are the masses. News Feeds are neutral, and if you use them stupidly, the News Feeds will act stupidly in return. The degree to which you overshare is the degree to which everyone else will butt in.

> tHe DeGree to WHicH you overSHare is tHe DeGree to WHicH everyone else Will Butt in.

That's like the fourth law of physics or something: To every immature Facebook status is an equal and opposite unwanted opinion from some nosy person in your News Feed, probably a relative. So make sure you share wisely; only a few people really care. The rest are just curious.

Facebook is neutral. It's not the enemy unless you make it the enemy. It is with social media as it is with all of life: you have to take the good and leave the rest.

Take the enjoyment, leave the addiction.

Take the communication, leave the isolation.

Take the inspiration, leave the jealousy.

> it iS WitH SOciaL meDia aS it iS WitH aLL OF LiFe; YOu Have to take the GOOD anD LeaVe tHe reSt.

YOUR FILTER

When I was a teenager, my mom taught me to read "with my filter on." She occasionally gave me books, poems, and articles with bad theology, questionable morals, or colorful language. She'd always attach a note that said something like, "I loved this paragraph," or "Her metaphors are stunning," or "It's a very interesting point of view," and she'd close with, "Read it with your filter on."

What she meant was, "I don't agree with everything in here, and you don't have to, either." Take the good and leave the rest. Stretch yourself, think critically, learn what you can—and let everything else fall by the wayside. Art doesn't have to fit nicely into your worldview to be valuable; neither do thoughts or opinions. What great loss I would have experienced if my mother had sheltered me from everything with which she didn't agree *entirely*. My mom gave me boundaries; she taught me the things that she believed to be unequivocally true, and then she filled my world with art and music and books and news articles and told me to drink it all in—with my filter on.

Aristotle wrote, "It is the mark of an educated mind to be able to entertain a thought without accepting it."

I hope your parents have given you a firm foundation. If they haven't, I'm sorry. I hope you have a church, a community, a mentor, or someone a little older and wiser to help you sort out the things that matter from the things that don't. I hope you've been intentional about figuring out what you believe, and not just floating through life with a "who knows, who cares" attitude. I hope you've developed a filter, so that you can dive into music and art and books without fear of being blown about, this way and that, by every good idea, every new perspective or argument. I hope you approach this great big world with your filter on. And I hope you approach the Internet—Facebook—through the filter of God's truth and wisdom.

Life isn't often all-or-nothing; you need to learn how to take the good and leave the rest. Let the Internet add to your life, not detract from it. Let it make you better, more connected. Use it to love people well, not to hoard likes and comments like a hungry bear going into hibernation. Facebook with your filter on.

Test everything. Hold on to the good. (1 Thessalonians 5:21)

THREE QUESTIONS

There are three questions that I use to determine whether or not a Facebook status (Twitter update, blog post, etc.) is worth posting. They aren't black and white, in fact, they're entirely subjective. No criteria, just questions. These three questions are my filter—my way to weed through my own thoughts and keep the best.

1. What story am I telling?

The nature of social media is that, through pictures and status updates, we get to write our own stories. People all over Facebook are telling the stories of their kids growing up, the places they go, the things they eat, the articles they read. The theme of your story is found in the common denominator of your posts: what do they have in common? What have you made your story about? Read through all of your statuses from the last three months and ask yourself, "What do all of my statuses have in common? What kind of story am I telling?"

> tHe nature OF SOCial meDia iS tHat, tHrOuGH PictureS anD StatuS uPDateS, We Get tO Write our OWn StorieS.

Are you telling a tragedy about all of your woes? (The weather is miserable, the homework load is impossible, your parents don't understand, your friends are fickle. All of these statuses usually end in ". . ." or "meh" or "siigghhhh.")

Are you telling a story about your emotions? (You're so happy! So in love! So angry. So betrayed. So sad. So overwhelmed. So confused.)

Are you telling a story about boys? (How much you love your boyfriend, how much you want a boyfriend, how that hot carhop at Sonic was checking you out.)

Most of your peers are telling the story of "WHAT I'M THINKING AND FEELING RIGHT NOW!!!" But Facebook is not a diary; it is a social media network. A social media network shared by bosses, colleagues, exes, prospective dates, teachers, parents, grandparents, and friends. The things we write in our diaries are our thoughts; the things we share on our Facebook profiles are our *stories*.

Ask yourself before posting, is what you're about to say worth contributing to the conversation? Will it help you to tell your story? The story you want to be telling?

2. If I went back and read all of my Facebook statuses, would I recognize me?

It is true that our heat-of-the-moment selves are not our best selves. We think for a split-second, "I cannot believe how many idiots are out there WHO DON'T USE THEIR TURN SIGNALS!" But we aren't angry people; we just had an angry moment. Is your News Feed filled with your angry moments? Your lonely or gossipy moments?

> it is true that our heat—of—the—moment selves are not our best selves.

Or is it a reflection of how beautiful you really are? Based on the things that you choose to share with the Internet, would you recognize yourself? Or would you think, *Wow, that girl sounds stressed.* In my experience, most teenagers would be forced to say, "That's not the real me; that's not the best me."

If you were to read about yourself, would you recognize yourself? Even more, would you like yourself? Choose to be your own friend? Would you trust yourself?

If not, why should anybody else?

3. If I went back and read all of my Facebook statuses, would I know that I was a Christian?

Jesus Christ is the most distinctive thing about me. My highest goal in life is to know Him and to make Him known, so if nobody who reads my Facebook wall could guess that I am a Christian, I'm not doing a very good job.

This is not to say that everything I post is about Jesus. In fact, most things are not. While the majority of what I write on my Facebook page is not about Jesus, I believe that everything there brings Him glory. I strive to live (and therefore post) in purity, humility, righteousness, love, and mercy. I endeavor to live and work in such a way that nothing I produce can malign the name of Christ.

If you were to tell your Facebook friends that you were a Christian, would they believe you?

When you can answer each of these questions positively, you can be sure that you are contributing something beautiful to the global conversation. Then Facebook, instead of a forum for passive-aggressive emotional rants, becomes what it is capable of being: a medium for connection, relationship, humor, encouragement, truth, and inspiration.

THINK IT THROUGH, TALK IT OUT

1. Have you ever seen a vague FB status and known it was about you?

2. Have you ever written a status and felt better after you posted it, because you needed to vent and be heard?

3. How does it make you feel when people like and comment on the things you post?

4. Take three minutes and try to imagine life without social media. How would your life be different? How would your relationships be different?

5. What story do your recent statuses tell?

6. What version of yourself do people on the Internet see? The exaggerator, the complainer, the relationship addict?

7. If you didn't know anything about yourself, and you could ONLY see the words in your status updates, would you recognize yourself? Would you want to be friends with yourself?

8. In what ways do you need to tweak your sharing habits to tell a better story? To reveal a truer version of yourself?

9. What does it mean to be intentional about the things you do and share online?

CHAPTER

4

VEGAN LIONS

"It is not necessary to react to everything you notice."[12]

I have unfortunate Eustachian tubes. Does anyone know what a Eustachian tube really is? I don't; all I know is that whenever I get a cold, they fill up with fluid and my ears punk out. My eardrums have ruptured a handful of times and are now so damaged that every time a doctor peeks in there he's all, "You know you're not supposed to stick Q-tips in that far, right?" My doctor told me that if my eardrums rupture again, I will start to lose my hearing—at the ripe age of twenty-seven. This is terrible information to give to a person who already jumps to the worst possible conclusions, medically speaking, because now, in my brain, the sniffles = certain deafness. And that doesn't even sound crazy to me because THE DOCTOR TOLD ME SO.

When I get the sniffles I go into DEFCON 1. I stop just short of pumping myself with intravenous fluids laced with echinacea. At the end of every day (during which I consume a vat of homemade organic chicken noodle soup and absolutely zero sugar or caffeine), my bedtime routine goes something like this:

Sudafed

Tylenol

Vitamin C

Zinc

Gargle with saltwater

(Piping) Hot herbal tea with honey

Chug apple cider vinegar

Steam shower

---

12. See http://www.aniotaoftruth.com/it-is-not-necessary-to-react-to everything-you-notice.

Vicks VapoRub

Cough drops

Saline nose spray

Fresh air

Sleep forever

Everything except for a Neti Pot because, "Know thyself." I know myself, and I would drown myself. Or I would forget to sterilize the water and end up with amoebas in my brain, which makes deafness seem like not such a big deal.

When I was pregnant with Henry, I got sick. After a week and a half of my two-hour bedtime routine, my ears were still fogging up. It sounded like I was underwater, or on an airplane; the time had come to seek professional help. For as much good as the Sudafed was doing, I may as well have been popping Red Hots every four hours, which at least would have tasted better.

I was sitting in the waiting room when an elderly woman got out her cell phone and made a call. She called her law office. I know this because the volume on her large-screen, large-button, old-person phone was so loud that I could clearly hear the clerk on the other end of the line.

The only thing more awkward than listening to her renegotiate her will, discuss her real estate properties, and disclose all sorts of personal financial information (including the full legal names of her grown children) was what happened next.

As soon as the elderly lady hung up her phone, a second woman (who shall henceforth be referred to as "The Aggressor") whipped around in her chair and said,

"There is not one single part of your brain that told you how completely inappropriate it was for you to have that conversation in here, huh!"

Yikes. There was no good way for the elderly lady to respond. The Aggressor made a statement, not a question. The Aggressor didn't speak out of concern, nor did she reprimand discreetly. She insulted the intelligence of a sweet old lady in front of a room full of people.

The elderly lady responded,

"I'm sorry, I can't hear you, sweetie. I guess everyone in here is so stuffed up with colds, hee hee hee. What did you say now, sweetie?"

All of us in the waiting room shoved our noses deep into our magazines and pretended not to hear The Aggressor repeat herself and threaten to go home and steal the elderly woman's identity—you know, to make a point.

Next, the elderly lady, still giggling, POLLED THE WAITING ROOM. Just, why? Let it go, people.

"Was anyone else bothered by my phone call? Who else here was bothered by my conversation? Hee hee hee."

I thought, *Surely, surely, there is not a third person in this waiting room crazy enough to get involved.*

Alas, I underestimated the human compulsion to get all up in other people's business. A third woman piped up and said, "Well, this was neither the time nor place . . ."

At which point I thought, *Forget it. I'm going home and going deaf.*

The point is, I sat there for fifteen minutes listening to three total strangers squabble and peck at each other in a doctor's office. As I watched this social microcosm unfolding, it occurred to me how much of the world's ugliness would be cured if we

> it occurred to me how much of the world's ugliness would be cured if we all just learned when to keep our mouths shut.

all just learned when to keep our mouths shut. Drama is not just a teen thing.

Drama is not a teen girl problem; it is a human problem. Drama is not something that everyone deals with and then outgrows, like acne. Drama is the fruit of ugly habits and bad manners, and there is no growing out, only growing up. When left unchecked, drama will follow you as long as you live, like a shadow, like a consequence. Just ask anybody in the workforce, or anybody trying to get a date, or anybody that volunteers at church. The world is full of people acting like eighth graders.[13]

The number of times you say, "I hate drama," is a pretty good indicator of how much you actually love drama. Non-dramatic people don't feel the need to discuss drama they didn't start and aren't involved in. Most of the time, the phrase "I hate drama" immediately follows a long, dramatic description of a dramatic incident, and sounds something like this:

> tHe numBer OF times you say, "i Hate Drama," is a pretty GOOD inDicator OF How mucH you actually love Drama.

> *"I am soooo not a dramatic person. I like hanging out with boys more than girls—girls are too dramatic. I hate drama so much. I am so sick of this drama! Will she just stop causing so much drama, like, it makes me so angry. Drama is stupid. Drama is ruining my life. I HATE DRAMA."*

Huh. Methinks the lady doth protest too much.[14]

---

13. No offense, if you are actually an eighth grader. You are allowed to act like an eighth grader if you are IN THE EIGHTH GRADE. After that, it's very unbecoming.
14. That's Shakespeare; you're welcome.

Look, I know there's a chance you actually do hate drama. It doesn't take a rocket scientist (or even an eighth-grade diploma) to see the mile-wide path of collateral damage that follows. But since when has a little collateral damage ever interfered with a girl's guilty pleasure? Gossip, flirtation, overspending, overeating—hating a thing doesn't usually stop us from doing it. You probably do hate drama, but you also probably dive in headfirst and splash around in the delicious, scandalous, emotional juiciness of it all.

I believe that the drama deck is stacked against you, as a teenage girl. That's not license to keep acting a fool, but it is an explanation. I mean, you're dramatic, but you're probably not crazy. You are contending with ruthless hormones, over-the-moon emotions, crushing insecurity, inevitable immaturity, and a bunch of blossoming opinions—all set in a culture of oversharing and "follow your heart" and "I don't care what anybody thinks about me." Throw a thousand of y'all into a confined space that has a social hierarchy in play (oh, there are also a thousand boys and half of them are cute), and what can we expect except for you to go absolutely tribal on one another? It's a wonder more physical injury isn't inflicted in the halls of our nation's high schools. We have to nip this in the bud, girls. Sure, I want you to live free and healthy lives, but mostly I want to minimize the chance that you'll end up on *Judge Judy* in your adulthood. This should be one of your highest ambitions: to stay off of any and all daytime television. Except for *The Price Is Right.* Because, free cars!

the epicenter of all your drama will always be longing.

While emotions and boys exacerbate the issue, the epicenter of all your drama will always be longing. It comes from inside, which is why you can't outgrow it and why, no matter how many times you say, "It's just this person, just this situation, just this whatever," it's not. It's in you, and getting it out has got to be an inside job.

VALIDATION: WHY I WATCH THE BACHELOR

The reason you are inclined to create drama is the same reason that I, a self-respecting adult with a college education, am inclined to watch *The Bachelor*. I hate *The Bachelor*. I hate the premise of the show, the gimmicks, the hokey rose ceremonies. I hate the prolonged suspense; I hate the mountains out of molehills and the anticlimactic cliff-hangers. I hate what it implies about love and romance and marriage. I hate what the fact that I watch *The Bachelor* says about me as a person. Every year I resolve, "I will not watch *The Bachelor*!" And every year I pull up an episode while I'm eating lunch (or painting my nails, or while Dan is working late), and I cannot stop. My friend Cindy understands; she once said, "It has reached the point in the season where I'm embarrassed that I watch this show." It was the third episode.

The reason I can't stay away? I like to judge people.

There, I said it. STOP JUDGING ME ABOUT IT!

Girls judging other girls is the driving force behind the success of this show. I am certain that the most-uttered phrases on Monday nights between 8:00 and 9:00 p.m. are:

"That is not real love."

"She's in it for the attention."

"I saw that coming a mile away."

"That is a codependent relationship waiting to happen."

"They will never last."

And the number one most commonly uttered phrase must be,

"That girl is insane," or the more colloquial, "That girl cray."

When we say these things, what we are really saying is, "I have insight! Look how right I am about this media-manufactured relationship!" It makes us feel wise, like we are more enlightened than all of those poor, beautiful women who have more hair extensions than they do common sense.

It is entertaining and validating, and it seduces us.

We are seduced by drama in the same way—because validation goes down so, so smoothly.

Just think: if you are longing to be heard, longing to be right—if you are longing to be smart enough or popular enough or liked enough—drama feels good.

It feels good to put your two cents in—to feel smart.

It feels good to offer your highly-evolved opinion.

It feels good to gain allies—to cocoon yourself with people who are loyal to you.

It feels good to pick sides—to stick up for somebody and to be stuck up for.

Drama garners a response, always, and it feels good to be responded to.

> Drama Garners a response, always, and it Feels Good to Be responDeD to.

When I'm not giving my children enough attention, they do things like uproot all my plants and eat handfuls of potting soil,[15] because that's what it takes to get me talking to them, even if I'm talking angrily. Kids know

---

15. This actually happened.

when they can get more attention with bad behavior than they can by being mannerly. And you are just a bunch of grown-up kids. We all are. You know, sometimes subconsciously, that even though the response to your drama might be gossip, outrage, or retaliation, negative attention is still attention.

> He who is full loathes honey, but to the hungry even what is bitter tastes sweet. (Proverbs 27:7)

The drama fallout is certainly bitter, but when you're starving for validation, even bitter drama tastes sweet.

STIMULATION: A POOR MAN'S PASSION

The second fundamental human longing at the source of your Oscar-worthy drama is passion.

Girls need adventure. Not just some of us, all of us. There is a wildness inside of every woman, a special kind of strength hiding in that second X chromosome. Loud or quiet, it's there.

My little girl is of the loud variety. She is five, and she approaches every area of her little life with abandon; she laughs, cries, runs, and loves with the intensity of the fire of a thousand suns. I spend all of my time talking Madeline off of cliffs—explaining to her that things are neither as terrible nor as monumental as she thinks. Madeline's favorite word is "ever." As in, "This is the tallest tower I've **ever** built! This is the best day I've **ever**

> There is a wildness inside of every woman, a special kind of strength hiding in that second X chromosome.

had! This is the best ice cream I've **ever** tasted! This is the worst tummy-ache I've **ever** felt! This is the meanest Sam has **ever** been! He took my favorite toy I've **ever** had and threw it harder than he's **ever** thrown!" I have a newborn and a two-year-old and 80 percent of my parenting effort *still* goes to Madeline, bringing her back to center. I don't know how that's even possible.

Madeline can change the world in the same way as Joan of Arc or Deborah the prophetess: Loud and bold and headlong.

My best friend, Brooke, is of the quiet variety. She quietly started her own business, and it quietly became a smashing success. She quietly handles big tasks and undertakes big ventures. She quietly carries big hurts and forgives big wrongs. She quietly lavishes generosity, and she quietly inspires thousands.

She is changing the world in the same way as Mother Teresa or Emily Dickinson. Softly, deeply, steadfastly—whether anyone notices right away or not.

A part of even the most staunch homebodies (of whom I am The Queen) fantasizes about adventure like Sacagawea's—leading men through the wilderness, strong, capable, and brave—the heroine of her own story. Our souls need passion—purpose. When we can't find it authentically, we manufacture it in the form of drama and daydreams to feed our hungry hearts. The problem is that you subsisting off of drama and daydreams is like a lion subsisting off of grass, berries, and bugs; you might survive, but you will never be healthy, and you will never be satisfied.

Girls crave adventure because we were created this way. God is on mission, and, as His followers, so are we. He has a plan for you, and the more I read through Scripture, the more likely it seems that it is not a safe plan.

Sarah left her life behind to follow her aging husband into some unknown "promised land" that she was just supposed to take on faith.

She also ended up having a baby when she was nearly one hundred years old. As someone who has had three babies, just let me say: Yikes.

Rahab looked armed guards square in the eye as they stood at her door, and lied to them—while harboring enemy spies.

Deborah led a battle. You guys, she LED A BATTLE.

Ruth knowingly settled in a hostile land and endured racial discrimination to preserve a relationship with her mother-in-law.

Esther went before the king on behalf of her people, knowing her beheading was likely. BEHEADING. As in, they chop off your head. Her cousin encouraged her, "Who knows but that you have come to royal position for such a time as this?" and Esther responded, "Go, gather together all the Jews . . . and fast for me. . . . I and my maids will fast as you do. When this is done, I will go to the king, even though it is against the law. And if I perish, I perish" (Esther 4:14–16).

That is a sense of purpose. If I perish, I perish. For such a time as this.

Life is a series of "for such a time as this" moments that are either seized, or not. Those of you that are out there seizing moments aren't involved in drama. Conversely, those of you that are entrenched in drama are never out there seizing moments. As I flip through the pages of my memory, looking back on all the teen girls I've had the privilege to know, I am amazed at the universality of this principle: girls that are training their backsides off for a spot on a traveling sports team, an athletic scholarship, or the Olympics aren't seduced by drama. Neither are girls that are organizing fund-raisers for cancer research or expending themselves to eradicate third world poverty. Career-minded teenagers that are job-shadowing executives and entrepreneurs don't have room for the emotional energy that drama requires.

Your soul knows that the world, time, *life* is about something bigger than yourself. When you feel disconnected from that, you will try to amplify your life to get just a taste of purpose. We are all so hungry for it. We spin, stir, and fret; we busy ourselves and we talk, talk, talk to get a whiff, a drip, just a morsel of connectedness to the bigness of God that our hearts are after. Farmers and sailors don't usually have drama; they are, by definition, connected to the bigness of God in a daily, tangible way. Earth, sky, sea. They are dependent on the God of the harvest, the God of the waves—star-breather, lightning-thrower, rain-sender, snow-storer, life-sustainer. As it happens, so are you, but it's easy to forget when you spend all day in class sitting at a tiny desk under fluorescent lighting.

> Your soul knows that the world, time, life is about something bigger than yourself.

We are mission people. Our hearts were created to be split wide open and to feel things. We were created to care about injustice in the world. We are on orders to care for widows, orphans, the poor, the hungry, and the persecuted. When those things begin to stir your heart, drama will dissipate like a vapor.

You crave purpose, but drama is easier.

You crave passion, but drama is easier.

You crave excitement, but drama comes much more naturally.

Drama is a poor girl's passion, a cowardly girl's creativity.

> Drama is an idle preoccupation; a cheap version of that which you really want, which is to live passionately on purpose.

Drama is stimulation without any of the higher purpose—with no great calling, with no burden burning a hole in your heart like a fire, with no risk, and no reward. Drama is an idle preoccupation; a cheap version of that which you really want, which is to live passionately on purpose.

If you are starving for validation and stimulation (and don't be afraid if you see this in yourself, I see it in myself almost constantly), you are a drama-risk. Insecure and bored is a recipe for disaster. But what happens when these natural, universal human longings are compounded by bad social habits? Armageddon? You wish. Babe, you will pray for fire and blood to rain from the sky, you will beg for earthquakes and floods and darkness and war and THE END OF ALL THINGS if God will please just spare you the consequences of the drama you've gone and meddled in. You'll be all wrapped up in a lose-lose situation where feelings and reputations and friendships are on the line, and the more you connive and spin and fret, the more hopelessly entrenched you'll become—like a little bug trying to squirm her way out of a spider web.

Bad social habits are catalysts that shift drama into *overdrive*. And habits, when ignored, etch themselves into our personalities by repetition, like a river steadily carving itself into a canyon.

Part of growing up, of becoming the most awesome version of yourself, is learning how to identify and shape your own habits—so pay attention.

There is a Cherokee legend that tells about a grandfather speaking to his grandson. He says to the boy, "There is a fight going on inside of every man and it is between two wolves. One wolf is evil: anger, hate, selfishness, pride, envy, and the other wolf is good: love, joy, peace, patience."

The grandson thinks for a moment, then asks, "Which one wins?"

The grandfather replies, "The one you feed."

Consider which of your habits shape you into a gracious human being, and feed those. Consider which habits don't, and work hard to starve them, before those relentless, repetitive waves of habit carve you up any more than they already have.

The bad habits that fuel the most cataclysmic, catastrophic drama are things like oversharing, overreacting, defensiveness, venting, and retaliation. These reactionary habits are learned—and they are very often learned from your mom.

BABY MAMA DRAMA

Women tend to be the primary managers of relationships in most families. We disproportionately care for children, aging parents, and keep in touch with friends. It is precious, rewarding work—to love people well, to invite them into our mess and to enter into theirs. It is also precarious work—peacemaking, discerning, communicating. Tending relationships must be done with consistency and grace; people must be handled with care. Take a look at the grown women in your life, all the major players and the caretakers around you. You are absorbing their social habits. Are you learning to handle people with care?

Once, when Dan and I were in full-time youth ministry, we had a family in our care that was so incredibly dysfunctional it defied statistics. It was like lightning struck their family tree in twelve different places. It was so improbable, for one family to be so dramatic. But they were.

A beautiful, precious teenage girl hailed from this family, whose behavior was neither beautiful nor precious. She was simultaneously insecure and callous, which she handled by retaliating at everything with sarcasm.[16] She interrupted, blame-shifted, and said things for shock value. She acted out for attention but insisted on privacy. She pursued independence yet demanded coddling. She handed out ultimatums like they were candy, and let friendships fall by the wayside when she didn't get her way. She overshared during prayer time, casually discussing all manner of private family problems: the ever-present threat of divorce, emotional abuse, and financial upheaval.

One afternoon we went to visit this girl at home, where we met her mother. Y'all—it was high school drama to the nth degree. The mother talked about her daughter like she wasn't STANDING RIGHT BESIDE HER. She tried to validate her parenting to us by saying things like, "I've tried to tell her . . ."

It was as if, with every passive-aggressive jab, she was saying, "It's not my fault she turned out like this!" We were so embarrassed for this poor girl, who had to stand there and listen to a catalog of her faults aired out like dirty laundry.

As our relationship with this family continued, the mother would often call the church for help and be offended if the church couldn't meet a given need. She volunteered private information under the guise of asking for prayer and blew up with anger any time she saw any kind of hypocrisy in her fellow church members.

It became clear to me that this teenage girl's behavior was not the inevitable amount of sass gifted to all tweens on their twelfth birthday by the Teen Sass Fairy. It was a collection of learned behaviors passed

---

16. Tip: too much sarcasm is not cute. It keeps people out like a force field. Use a little. Be clever and fun and whatever, but err on the side of kind. Err on the side of authentic. Out-sarcasm-ing someone is not the same as out-smarting or out-funny-ing or out-cute-ing them. Too much sarcasm makes you really annoying to talk to.

down from her parents who never learned how to rise above the chaos: entitlement, insecurity, passive aggression, and a loose tongue.

At first glance, this family seemed to have been dealt an unfair hand—so many difficulties to overcome. But upon closer inspection, a large part of their trouble was a direct consequence of their drama. The universe wasn't out to get them; their habits were.

If the greatest culprits for drama are impulses—emotional reactions and immature reasoning, then the greatest weapons against drama are decisions—perspective, grace, and self-control.

When your family is late and stuck in an excruciatingly slow drive-through line only to have your order butchered, how do your parents react?

Do they vent, shred the service up one side and down the other, or blame you for changing your clothes four times and insisting that you HAD to flat-iron your hair before you left "BECAUSE WHAT IF WE'RE IN A CAR ACCIDENT AND THE MEDIC IS REALLY HOT?!??! I can't have frizzy hair for my hot medic future husband!"? If they do, that's okay—don't crucify them, but don't imitate them, either. The most successful people don't have things happen to them; they happen to things. So go happen to your habits. Don't let them happen to you; don't absorb a sense of entitlement, blame-shifting, and the inability to hold your tongue just because that's how your parents act.

> iF tHe GreateSt CuIpritS For Drama are impulSeS—emotional reactionS anD immature reaSoninG, tHen tHe GreateSt WeaponS aGainSt Drama are DeciSionS—perSpective, Grace, anD SeIF—control.

If, in the drive-through line, you see your mother withhold judgment (perhaps the kitchen is short-staffed), extend the benefit of the doubt (perhaps the server is surviving a terrible day), and muscle through a frustrating situation, take note and be thankful—you are absorbing a temperedness and graciousness that will stop drama in its tracks.

If you come from a long line of temper-losers or sneaky manipulators, you can be the one to end the cycle. You can open your eyes, see your habits for what they are and what they do, and choose a better way.

Here is a one-minute primer on how to damper the drama in your life:

Assume everyone is doing the best they can. Offer the benefit of the doubt. Mind your own business. Mind your manners. Choose your battles. Don't take it so personally; eliminate defensiveness. Evaluate: am I speaking to help? Or speaking to make myself feel better? Be humble. Be gracious. Don't believe everything you think. To the extent you control your temper and your tongue, you control your life. Wage war on jealousy; you are enough. Refuse bitterness—stiff-arm it. Don't react; respond. If you take pleasure in correcting someone, that is the time to hold your tongue; if it pains you, that is the time to speak in love. Don't let your mood affect your character. Think bigger—pray for perspective. Practice empathy. Love people, love people, just love people.

The hopeful thing about habits is that, just as they can be learned, they can be unlearned. It's never too late. Years of snap judgments and emotional outbursts are no match for God's ability to transform. Do not underestimate the power of radical self-discipline and of grace. Eliminate dramatic responses from your behavior and watch the drama around you float off, like a morning fog.

> tHE HOPEFUl tHiNG aBOUt HaBitS iS tHat, JUSt aS tHEY caN BE learNED, tHEY caN BE uNIearNED.

LET THEM EAT BAGELS

My mom was a Sunday school teacher once, for a fledgling little church full of friends. One morning, as she was preparing her first-grade lesson around the kitchen table, she looked to me and said, "Kate, I'm going to teach these little ones to pray. They are not too young to put their theology into practice. I'm going to give them SUSTENANCE in the morning! Marie Antoinette said, 'Let them eat cake,' but I say, 'Let them eat BAGELS!'" Then she thrust her fist into the air like she was leading the metaphorical bagels into battle.

"Let them eat bagels" became an instant catchphrase in our home. Whenever we talked about something of real importance, something we knew way down deep in our knowers, the most sustaining, truest of things, we would say, "This is the real stuff of life; this is bagels!"

I use drama to feed my hungry human heart. So do you—we all do. So to quell the drama, put something better on your plate. Don't eat berries, little lion, eat meat. Don't eat cake; eat bagels.

If you want to *matter*—if you want to be heard, to affect something, to be included and involved, you are hungry for validation. Consider where you are finding your value. Consider what God says about you— that every day of your life was written in His book before it came to be, that He sees you and knows you and loves you. Remember that you are good at stuff; that God knitted a personality into you and gave you all sorts of gifts so that you could go do amazing things. Remember the things He promised—that you will be able to do even greater things than the apostles in the early church did! You are interesting, and you matter.

If you recognize in yourself a hunger for validation, pay close attention to the people who value you. Find someone to talk to that really listens to you. Real, eye-contact, mm-hmming, *listens*. Find a community of believers that values you for who you are—not for the juicy information you have or the extraordinary stories you can tell. Find a sweet group of friends that will laugh and cry and scheme and giggle and daydream about boys with you—girls that love and value you—and girls that will commit WITH YOU to avoid drama. When I was in the ninth grade, one of my best friends was a girl named Esther. One day, we were standing in front of my locker and I started to tell her about . . . I don't know . . . someone. I never got to finish my sentence because before I even got to the point, Esther stopped me short and said, "Kate, I don't think we should be talking about this." You guys—she was right and I am so thankful for her courage to stop me. I didn't even realize it was happening, but she did. I laughed harder with Esther than I did with almost anyone. We pranked people together, we talked about boys together, we shopped and exercised and went to the beach together. We also went to Bible study together. Esther left encouraging notes in my locker, and she helped me to avoid gossip and drama. If you don't have a best friend like that, find one, STAT.

If you are addicted to the high of drama, if you zero in on the excitement, the preoccupation, the titillation, you are hungry for stimulation. This is you if you love overhearing classmates talk about their personal lives. If you can't wait to get together with your friends and speculate about why so-and-so did such-and-such. If you want to compare notes with your friends about who saw what and what it means, you are hungry for stimulation. You need something to fascinate and captivate you, and if you don't find something worthwhile fast, you'll waste the better part of your teenage years making pointless guesses about your classmates' social lives.

If you are hungry for stimulation, the best way to feed yourself is to challenge yourself. Being busy is not enough. Sometimes adults say "idle hands are the devil's playthings," but I don't think that's entirely true. Aren't the girls who are in every club and on every team some of the most dramatic people you know? Being on a cheerleading team won't keep anyone out of drama, just ask, oh, ANYBODY WHO'S EVER BEEN TO HIGH SCHOOL—but *loving* cheering enough to assume some extra responsibility, to choreograph for a competition, to really pursue it, might. Idle hands aren't the problem; idle hearts are. Busyness is not a drama deterrent; passion is.

> Busyness is not a drama deterrent; passion is.

Open your heart to the plight of orphans, the homeless, the hungry, the persecuted, the enslaved, or even the hurt and need among your peers, and drama won't seduce you. The excitement of drama can't hold a candle to the excitement of a cause, a calling. When we stack drama up against the epic story of the real world, we see it for what it really is: petty, idle, divisive, and worthless.

Passion and adventure work like force fields against drama; idle words and worries get zapped by their extravagant hope and possibility. Maturity is not boring or lesser—it's greater. Listen, if you get sucked into the drama trap too easily, all you have to do is bust out of your everyday routine—get out of the little box you're in—and open up your eyes to what's real.

> The excitement of drama can't hold a candle to the excitement of a cause, a calling.

Crack the door and let all of broken, beautiful humanity flood in like a sunbeam. Go spend a Saturday at a homeless shelter, or go cheer on some marathon runners—the exhaustion and emotion at the finish

line will astound you. Go play with some kids in a neighborhood that scares you a little, go deliver groceries to a single mom. Go on a mission trip overseas, attend a march to end modern-day slavery; you won't be able to un-see it. Let it in; let it move you. Let it inspire you, wreck you, challenge you. Let it change you. If you want to catch the fire, you're going to have to get near the flame.

We settle for gossip and Facebook News Feeds because they're occupying and engaging. But we're hungry. We are vegan lions in a constant state of craving, and at the first whiff of meat (or bagels) our breath will catch in our chests and we'll know: "THIS, this is what I've been hungry for my whole life." Connection to the bigness, to God, to eternal things, to the mission. Ann Voskamp wrote, "We are hungry for hard and holy things because we want more than hollow lives." Yes.

God wasn't lying when He said that He owns the cattle on a thousand hills. He wasn't lying when He said that, with the Holy Spirit inhabiting us, we would do greater things than even the apostles in the early church were able to do. He was not lying when He said that He would be with us as we go to the uttermost parts of the earth. He was not lying when He said He would replace our heart of stone with a heart of flesh. He was not lying when He said that He was a consuming fire, that He would give us the nations as our inheritance, that He came to give us life to the fullest.

Do you not believe Him? Do you think He was speaking figuratively? Well, He wasn't. So get excited. Get on mission. Get in love.

Forget drama; it's a total waste of time. It makes you sound petty, and it hurts more people than it's ever helped. If you find a group of friends that plays with you and prays with you, and together you dive headfirst into something exciting and meaningful, you will never settle for something as dumb as drama ever again.

THINK IT THROUGH, TALK IT OUT

1. On a scale of 1–10, how much drama is in your school? What about in your group of friends?

2. What parts of drama do you kind of enjoy, and what parts do you hate?

3. Have you ever been the victim of drama?

4. Kate talked about being hungry for validation (to be heard, right, liked, acknowledged, and to matter) and hungry for stimulation (to be involved, interested, excited, invested, and wrapped up in something). Do you think you are hungrier for validation or stimulation? Why?

5. What would your life look like if you fell passionately in love with Jesus?

6. What social habits do you see yourself absorbing from the grown women around you? Are they mostly good or mostly bad? How can you be intentional about the social habits you are forming?

7. Which sounds more fulfilling to you: drama or passion? Why do we choose drama over passion so often?

8. What are some easy, practical things you and your friends can do to avoid hurtful drama?

9. Eleanor Roosevelt said, "Great minds discuss ideas, average minds discuss events, small minds discuss people." How can you shift the dialogue among your group of friends?

CHAPTER 5

A PACK OF WOLVES IS NATURAL

"Sometimes I'm terrified of my heart, of its constant hunger for whatever it wants. The way it stops and starts." -Poe, singer/songwriter

"That's where the truth lies, right down here in the gut. Do you know you have more nerve endings in your gut than you have in your head? You can look it up. Now, I know some of you are going to say, 'I did look it up, and that's not true.' That's 'cause you looked it up in a book. Next time, look it up in your gut. I did." -Stephen Colbert

"Follow your heart" is terrible, stupid, awful advice. The worst.

It is the worst because it DOES NOT TRANSLATE. When people say "Follow your heart," they probably mean one of the following:

"Do you know this is right?"

"Can you do this with a clear conscience?"

"Is this wise, long-term? Is this what you really want?"

"Do you really like him?"

"Is this something you truly care about?"

All of which are excellent questions. But when you *hear* "Follow your heart," you probably think:

"If I want to do something, I should do it, because my heart is telling me to."

"Everything is a sign."

"If I'm doubting my commitment to something, my heart is not in it."

"If I want to make out with a boy in his car in my driveway before he drops me off for curfew—if there is undeniable chemistry—that's my heart telling me that we have something special."

"Whatever I want is right for me, and if (INCONCEIVABLY) I end up making a stupid mistake, it's okay because it was a crime of passion; I was following my heart."

"My heart will not lead me astray."

But all the women who ever dated a thirty-year-old man that lived with his parents or was addicted to Call of Duty or used too much Axe body spray or didn't know how to fold his own laundry or thought that Taco Bell was a legit option for Mexican food-date night will tell you— YOUR HEART CAN LEAD YOU ASTRAY.

A lot of girls before you have followed their hearts right into a cult or a pyramid scheme or a dead-end, codependent relationship because it "felt right." You know that warm, tingly feeling you get all over your body when you see a boy you like? That's common sense leaving your body. That itchy, eager feeling you get right before you let somebody have a piece of your mind is common sense evacuating your bloodstream. And that floating, invincible euphoria you feel when you're about to take a stupid risk is common sense ACTUALLY EVAPORATING off of your skin.

We tend to believe that if a thing is natural, it must be right. That premise sneaks its way into our system of beliefs, and we honor it without even thinking. Just look around: the marketing departments of every food, cosmetic, and cleaning supply industry are engaged in a who's-more-natural-than-who battle that has escalated to epic proportions. The last time I was in the grocery store I could practically hear the jars of peanut butter shouting across the aisle at each other:

"I have no preservatives!"

"Well, I have no high fructose corn syrup!"

"Well, I am made of peanuts and salt—no added ingredients!"

"Well I am made with organic, locally-grown peanuts, hand-picked in the United States by celibate priests who washed their hands with sulfate-free castile soap and filtered water—AND KOSHER SEA SALT."

The obsession with natural is fine when it comes to keeping chemicals out of your body, but it's not a universal principle. Natural does not always mean safe, or smart, or right. As comedian Matt Kirshen says, "They say, 'It's safe; it came from the earth. It's natural.' Heroin is natural. Nicotine is natural. A pack of wolves, the edge of a cliff. What else? Look, I got you this big grumpy bear! Don't worry, he's organic!"

This is my go-to cautionary word to you if you are into following your natural heart-feelings. "Oh, you can't help yourself? It's chemistry, is it? It's natural? A PACK OF WOLVES IS **NATURAL**, SUZIE."

It's especially effective when I shout it with crazy eyes. Maybe spit a little.

The same faulty reasoning is why some of you justify gossip and cruelty by saying, "Well, it's *true.*" Girls, stop acting like this kind of truth-telling is your act of service to humanity. You say, "I'm just an honest person," or "I call it like I see it," or "I'm just saying what everyone else is thinking." Honey, the reason no one else is saying it is because they had enough decency to keep their mouths shut. Whatever you're saying may be true, but I'm sure there are a lot of things that are true about you that you wouldn't want me to tell all my friends.

Just because a thing is true, doesn't mean it's necessary. Not all truths are kind or loving or anybody's business. Our standard for speech isn't truth; it's love.[17]

Our choices are subject to a similar set of standards. There is natural, and then there is *right.* Just because a thing is natural doesn't mean it's healthy or safe. The standard for our behavior isn't what's natural; it's what's wise.

> JUST BECAUSE A THING IS TRUE, DOESN'T MEAN IT'S NECESSARY.

---

17. "Do not let any unwholesome talk come out of your mouths, but only what is helpful for building others up" (Ephesians 4:29).

Jeremiah 17:9 says, "The heart is more deceitful than anything else, and incurable—who can understand it?" (HCSB).

Deceptive, incurable, incomprehensible. Yeah, *what could go wrong?*

The next time someone tells you to follow your heart, you need to say, "Oh, you mean my wicked, deceptive, incurable, incomprehensible cardiovascular pump? The symbolic center of all my impulses and whims and selfishness? No thanks, I'M GOOD."

I'm not saying that you have to be a robot or a conformist or some sort of boring, risk-assessment professional with a spreadsheet. In fact, I agree with the spirit behind "follow your heart"—just not the practical applications. It's not specific enough advice; people abuse and misuse it more than they get it right. I'll never tell you to follow your heart. I'll tell you to follow your passions, your dreams, your skills, your opportunities, your brain, your intuition, and your Savior—but for crying out loud, and for your own sake, never, ever your heart.

BETTER THINGS TO FOLLOW

Passion

When you follow your heart, you'll pursue what you want now. If you follow your passion, you'll pursue what you want most. The difference will change your life. I enjoy thrift shopping. I enjoy puttering around my house, blogging, and keeping in touch with old friends. But when I sponsored a little six-year-old girl in Brazil, I told my husband, "This feels like the most worthwhile thing I've done all year."

I love leading small groups, building relationships, and teaching, but I cry when people tell me about selling their cars and homes and furniture and moving across the globe because Christ is worth it. Because His glory and the souls of men are worth it.

I have an opinion about immigration laws, foreign aid, marriage equality, and tax laws. But I openly wept when I read *Horton Hears a Who* as an adult, because "a person's a person, no matter how small." The value of human life, no matter the level of ability or disability, moves me to tears. Foster parents make me cry. Adoption makes me cry. Special needs professionals and ministries make me cry in the best way.

We should pay careful attention to the things that make us cry.

In Greek, the word for "passion" is the same word used for "suffering," which I think is telling and beautiful. Louie Giglio once said, "Passion is the degree of difficulty you're willing to endure to get to the stuff that matters." Exactly. How hard you are willing to fight for something is a good indicator of how passionate you are about it. If you're willing to endure long hours, painstaking attention to detail, long practices, criticism, teasing—if you're willing to let other opportunities pass you by in order to keep doing this thing you love—that might be passion. You might be passionate about art, music, a sport, a hobby, or a cause—those are the things to follow.

If you follow your heart, you'll pursue your hobby until it gets hard. You'll keep dancing or singing or playing until you get bored with the technicalities and you don't want

> HOW HArD YOU are WilliNG to FiGHt For SOMEtHiNG iS a GOOD inDicator OF HOW PaSSionate YOU are aBOUt it.

to go to practice anymore. You will interpret your disinterest or lack of motivation as your "heart" telling you it isn't worth it. That is one of the heart's great deceptions—telling us that things aren't worth it. But if they are passions, of course they are. Our hearts seek the path of least resistance, and I never want you to know the profound sense of loss you'll experience if you look back and see wasted years—all the times you followed what you wanted "now" instead of what you wanted most.

Follow your passions. Let the people who love you help you see them when your weary heart has lost sight of them. Push through the hard and the monotonous to the place where it gets really, really good. Nothing good ever comes easy, and if you're following your heart, you'll never know passion because you'll never endure the suffering it takes to get there. Your heart will take you into the shallows, full of splashing and play and frivolity. Passion will take you out past the breakers—into a deep ocean of awesome.

Dreams

There is an old Christian adage that says, "Bloom where you're planted." I guess that's fine in that we should serve Christ wherever we are, right this very minute. But when I hear it I can't help but think, *Who says I've been planted?* I am not a shrub. I am a person. I believe in doing the next right thing, and in doing what you can for who you can with what you have—so if that's what people mean by "bloom where you're planted," I guess I can get on board. But more often than not, I hear people passing down this little pearl when a girl is dreaming. One of your parents might tell you to bloom where you're planted if you want to spend a year abroad, or go on a mission trip to Indonesia, or go to college in New York—basically anything new and scary. They'll say it because they love you. They'll say it because they want to make sure you're not being impulsive—to make sure you've thought through all of the implications.

You should listen to them, talk it out, honor them, and trust that they can see a little bit further down the road than you can—BUT THEN, after you talk and think and pray and look down the road with them, if you just can't stop dreaming the dream—go for it. Ask your parents for their blessing, their help, their support, and go for it—all in.

Dreams are birthed out of passions; they are full of hope and possibility. Your dreams represent your preferred future. They represent the best, most-awakened versions of you—and they are worth pursuing. The most successful people on earth are dreamers. Big-dreaming is a skill that can be learned and should be practiced. Leaders think big (then a little bigger, then a little bigger). It takes lots of guts to be a dreamer because the risk of disappointment is so high. It takes discipline to set the bar high and work your tail off to reach it, believing all the while. Faith is not for the faint of heart.

> Dreams represent the best, most-awakened versions of you—and they are worth pursuing.

The most fulfilled people out there are the ones who turned their dreams into realities—into careers and habits and lives. The dream may cost a lot, but that's your cost to measure, and, a lot of times, it's worth it. Your dreams might be enormous; they might be God-sized, and if they are also God-honoring, you can believe that He's in them. I need dreamers to challenge me. Our world needs girls with vision and guts and discipline. We need girls full of optimism, determination, fire, and hope. We need big, out-of-the-box thinkers. We need you. Don't follow your heart; it will only lead you as far as your own self-interest. Your dreams, however, might just change the world.

Skills

You are gifted. Maybe you've been a standout in a particular area since you could walk, or perhaps you're still discovering and developing what will be your greatest skill set. You will definitely have a spiritual gift, plus a bunch of natural strengths and weaknesses, and they all intermingle to create a person-pattern that is only yours. I imagine personalities like equalizers—the little red and green bars of light that move up and down on the soundboards at recording studios. God is the great cosmic mixer, the brilliant engineer of personalities: dialing gifts, skills, and proclivities up and down.

I have the spiritual gift of encouragement, but I'm also an introvert. I'm over-the-top organized, but often messy, because I have ZERO self-discipline. None. I have a little bit of a teaching gift in that I like school, writing, and communicating—but research bores me, and I lack the insatiable curiosity that usually accompanies that gift. My optimism and enthusiasm is childlike: unrelenting, which is sweet but also irritating, especially if you're not in a great mood. I'm not the same as the other encouragers or the other teachers. I have interests and character traits that mix with my gifts and talents, and the output is Kate. It makes me perfectly suited for what I do.

> GOD IS THE GREAT COSMIC MIXER, THE BRILLIANT ENGINEER OF PERSONALITIES: DIALING GIFTS, SKILLS, AND PROCLIVITIES UP AND DOWN.

You are perfectly suited for something too. If you want to know what it is, pay attention to the opportunities you're offered. What do people notice about you? What do people ask you to help with? What jobs, positions, and opportunities do people offer you because *you* came to mind? The opportunities you're offered are a good indicator of where your strengths and gifts lie.

Instead of following your heart, step through the doors that are opened to you. Don't worry about "Is this the best choice? Is this God's will for my life? What if I miss out on something else because I'm busy doing this? What if I can't handle this, what if I mess it up?" God is involved and concerned with the intimate details of your life—of your days. I know that He guides and protects, and that means that you'd have to blow through some serious roadblocks to keep walking down a path that wasn't right for you.

This frees you to step through open doors, to walk into opportunities without the paralyzing fear of, "Is this the right thing to do?" If it's wrong, God will make it clear. He will make it clear through the Holy Spirit speaking to your soul, through your conscience. He will make it clear through His Word, through closed doors, obstacles, and sound advice from people that know and love you. If you veer off course, God will stop you short; He'll redirect. The Good Shepherd always comes for us when we wander. So if there is an opportunity that appeals to your talents—your gifts, skills, or desires—take it! Say yes; see where it takes you.

I was in the seventh grade when, to my astonishment, my parents said "yes" to a two-week exchange trip to France. I was twelve years old when I brought home a flyer that had a picture of the palace of Versailles on it. Below was the time and date of an interest meeting—and my parents said yes. I was afraid of not knowing the language and of staying alone in a house with a host family, but my parents prepared me and reassured me. That trip (which was based on my interests, skills, and opportunities) opened my eyes to the world outside of Raleigh, North Carolina. It opened me up to travel, independence, and a great love of languages, cultures, and people that are different from me. In hindsight, it shaped me in the best way. I love the things I learned there, and the things that trip forged in me.

In the face of God-ordained opportunities, you might still feel scared—that's your incurable heart. Your heart might also feel lazy or short-sighted, but your skills and opportunities will lead you well. Be brave; say

> Dare to watch your
> life unfold in beautiful
> and unexpected ways.

"yes." Dare to watch your life unfold in beautiful and unexpected ways. Don't let things happen to you; you go happen to things. Keep taking the next step. It is in the surprises that you'll learn about all the ways God has gifted you. And you'll see, every day, that He delights to give you good things.

Brain

You have a brain. That brain works pretty well; it's been keeping you alive for more than a decade now. It reminds you not to put your hands on stoves or jump into pools with your phone in your pocket. That brain of yours has a decent track record, and it's high time you started listening to it when it gives you advice about stuff.

It's easy to tell how often you are or aren't listening to your brain; just listen to how many of your sentences begin with disclaimers. The more disclaimers you use, the less you're listening to your brain. Your brain is in charge of logic and reason, so if you're constantly rationalizing and preempting your actions, you're obviously not acting logically. If you start a sentence with, "No offense, but . . ." your brain is telling you, "The thing you're about to say is offensive. Stop, stop, stop, stop, stop . . ."

If you say to your mother, "I know you said such-and-such, but . . ." your brain is telling you, "You are disregarding something you've been told. Give it up."

If you have to rationalize something, it's because your brain is telling you, "This is a bad idea." The worst, most hilarious, stupidest argument I've ever had with my brain was the summer before I left for college. Just out of a serious, heartbreaking relationship with my high school sweetheart, I'd been spending more and more time with a good friend of mine, as he was one of the only people still speaking to me after the breakup went down. One night, we were in his car, and I could tell he was going to kiss me. He was an honorable guy; he respected me, and we'd been good friends for a long time, so I wasn't in any danger, but I knew I didn't like him romantically.

> iF YOU HaVe to rationalize SometHinG, it's Because YOUR Brain iS tellinG YOU, "this iS a BaD iDea."

I knew I never wanted to date him. I knew that I didn't REALLY want to kiss him, and I definitely didn't want to have all of the uncomfortable conversational fallout after the kiss. Those are all the things my brain told me. My brain said, "You do not like this boy. You are not attracted to this boy. You are leading this boy on. You are ruining your friendship with this great, great boy. Get out. EARTH TO KATE: YOU DO NOT EVEN LIKE THIS BOY!"

Then my heart retorted with the most idiotic argument ever. It said, "But you're seventeen. This is what seventeen-year-olds do. What if you make it to eighteen without ever kissing a boy you shouldn't? You have to kiss him so that you can make a mistake. "

And do you know what? I DID IT. I kissed him like an ever-loving idiot listening to her wicked, incurable, incomprehensible heart instead of her brain with the good track record. The fallout was awkward and awful. In fact, it was so awful that I only kissed two boys after that—and I married one of them. I still feel like an insensitive fool when I think about it. And don't give me any slack; don't say, "You were only seventeen." That's the reasoning that got me into trouble in the first place. Seventeen-year-olds can know better; I did.

Listen to your brain! Logic, reason, and common sense are all better things to follow than your heart. Hearts will tell you to kiss boys (that you don't even like) in cars late at night. Hearts will tell you to make mistakes (and hurt people) just for the fun of it. It's okay to make mistakes, as long as they are mistakes. But if your brain tells you, "This is a stupid idea! Don't do this!" and you do it anyway, that's not a mistake; that's a fully cognitive choice. An immature decision. Use your brain; it has kept your hands away from open flames and kept your phone out of bodies of water—it has kept you out of trouble, which, I'm sure, is more than you can say about your heart. Every time I've ever been in trouble—every time I've made a terrible choice (some of which had consequences that changed my life forever), I was following my heart. And, in hindsight, I can see all the ways I could have been spared if I'd listened to my brain a little bit more.

Intuition

Intuition is a real thing, straight up. Discernment is a spiritual gift. I believe in good vibes and bad vibes, and I believe they can save your life. Intuition is more subjective than logic or reason, but be careful not to dismiss it, especially if you are someone who sees the world in black and white instead of in shades of gray. Here is what you need to know about intuition:

If you are getting bad vibes from a guy, get out—fast. Do not spend even sixty more *seconds* thinking about a polite or discreet way to get out, just get out.

If you are getting bad vibes about a job, don't take it. If an opportunity strikes you as shady, or a deal seems too good to be true, let it go.

If you get bad vibes about a friend, don't confide in her. If you get bad vibes about a church or a ministry, feel the freedom to leave.

Intuition, I believe, is based on a collection of subconscious observations: body language, tone of voice, atmosphere. When there are coincidences or motives that we can't reconcile, something doesn't sit right, we can feel it. Dr. Joyce Brothers said it this way: "Trust your hunches. They're usually based on facts filed away just below the conscious level." Women, as a group, tend to be more in tune with relational, social, and emotional subtleties than men are, so some of us have razor-sharp intuitions, a real sixth sense. You are developing your sixth sense, so never rationalize away a bad feeling that you just can't shake. Intuition is real, and it's okay to trust it.

Intuition is also a helpful thing to heed when it comes to talking (versus holding your tongue). If you want to say something, but your intuition tells you that maybe, just maybe you shouldn't—don't. If you want to let someone have it, but your breath catches for just a second— stop. If you want to share something private, but you wonder for just a second if it's too much—wait. If you suspect that what you want to say might come across as bragging (or complaining, or critical, or hurtful)—stop. Share it another time and in another way.

> never rationalize away a bad feeling that you just can't shake. intuition is real, and it's okay to trust it.

Intuition won't just keep you from bad things; it can also prompt you to act positively. It can move you toward other people when they, or you, need it most. If you notice someone sitting alone at lunch and you feel a tugging—go sit with them. If someone is new to church or school or a team and you think—even for a second—*I should invite her over,* you're right; you should. If you suspect someone might need help, encouragement, or a friend, you should do it, even if it seems out of the blue. Even if it doesn't make sense, and you're afraid of seeming weird or creepy—just do it.

If you know someone whose parents are going through a divorce, or someone who's going through a tough breakup; someone who has suffered a loss or is grieving in some way, and you want to say something, you should. You should say, "I love you," or "I'm sorry," or even "I don't know what to say." But don't ignore it because it's tender or uncomfortable. If you suspect that God wants you to reach out to someone, you do it. If you can't stop thinking about the homeless family on the corner, go give them some money, or a warm meal. If you can't stop thinking about the elderly lady at the park, go strike up a conversation with her. We are relational beings, and (when your hormones and pheromones aren't muddling things up) intuition is great at telling you if someone is in need of connection, or if they are bad news.

Intuition is meant to help you choose between two good options—**not** to choose between a good option and a bad one. If you are stuck between two great jobs, use your intuition. Whichever one feels the best to you, go for it. If you are blessed enough to get to choose between two great colleges, by all means, go with your gut! If you're waffling between two stand-up guys that are both pursuing you (lucky dog), intuition is the way to go. But if one guy is really kind and the other is kind of a jerk? Forget intuition and forget your heart—you need to follow the voices of all the women who have gone before, because, we know, sweetie. WE KNOW.

The principle is the same now and forever; it is true for me and for your grandparents and for the President of the United States: if one choice has a long list of cons, if everyone you trust is cautioning against it, and some curious, gutsy part inside of you still wants to give it a shot—don't. If one choice is wise and the other is not, you don't need to think about it anymore. No praying or fasting required. If you are faced with a good choice versus a bad one, God begs you to choose the good. "I have set before you life and death, blessing and curse. Choose life . . ." (Deuteronomy 30:19 HCSB).

Choose life. Choose health. Choose wisdom. Choose self-control. Listen to reason, to common sense, and your brain. No intuition required.

GOD'S WORD

Sometimes, I freeze.

When twelve things need to happen at once and each one is dependent on the others—when there is no right order, no efficient course of action, I feel like I can't move my extremities. My brain locks up and I feel simultaneously overstimulated and paralyzed—hearing everything and affecting nothing.

For me, it happens most often when it's 6:00 p.m., I have no dinner plan, the house is a disaster, all three kids are screaming, the baby needs to be nursed, Madeline has homework, and everyone needs to be in bed in ninety minutes (this happens at least twice a week). For you, it might be when you need to turn in college applications, switch your hours at work, finish your senior anthology project, and you have a concert, a football game, a party, small group, church, yearbook deadlines, babysitting, three tests, a paper, and a mound of homework big enough to die under.

My mantra when I get frozen and overwhelmed is this: "When you don't know what to do, do what you know to do."

It is my mantra when I feel aimless, like whatever mystical thing that holds my thoughts together like

WHEN YOU DON'T KNOW WHAT TO DO, DO WHAT YOU KNOW TO DO.

skin is gone, and I'm dissipating, drifting away from myself. When simple choices feel like advanced calculus, I recite, "Just do what you know to do."

Deep breath, one foot in front of the other.

In my frozen 6:00 p.m.'s, what I know to do is to pick a child, any child, and hug it. I can't fix all the hurts, but I can fix one. Next, I clear one little corner of a room to function as a sanctuary; I throw armfuls of toys and laundry and trash into a hamper and shove it out of sight, wrap the babies in blankets, and sit them in the sanctuary with juice boxes. In clearing a space I clear my brain. My living room and my brain are connected in a mystical, spiritual way. When one is clean, so is the other—and vice versa. When I don't know what to do, I just do something—anything—that I know is right. I nurture something. Clean, fix, and solve something. Anything.

For you, it might be to do homework for one class—just one. Just to be able to cross one thing off of the to-do list. Just make one phone call. Just do the next right thing.

This principle—doing what you know to do—works on a grand scale as well as it does on a daily 6:00 p.m. scale.

The Bible, the Word of God, tells us what is right in every situation. It speaks to our actions, words, thoughts, and attitudes—it addresses our whole selves and how those selves interact with the world around us. Whether we are frozen or floating, we can pick something, anything, that God tells us is right and do it.

When you don't know what to do, it is better to follow Scripture than it is to follow your passions, your dreams, your skills, your brain, your intuition, or anything else. Scripture is the only safe choice.

There are so many decisions, so many crises, inherent in adolescence—it will be one of the most defining periods of your life.

Middle school and high school are filled with watershed moments, magic moments, where a simple "yes" or "no" will change your world forever. So when you come to one of the million moments in which you don't know what to do, it is essential that you be grounded in the Word of God.

> MIDDLE SCHOOL AND HIGH SCHOOL ARE FILLED WITH WATERSHED MOMENTS, MAGIC MOMENTS, WHERE A SIMPLE "YES" OR "NO" WILL CHANGE YOUR WORLD FOREVER.

Prepare yourself for the frozen moments by memorizing scriptural truths that are always right, no matter what. Then, when you don't know what to do, just do what you know to do. Consider what the Bible tells you is right and good, and pick one:

Pray. Give to the poor. Forgive someone. Trust Jesus. Love God with your whole self. Get baptized. Love all people. Share your possessions. Tithe. Take care of other believers. Care for widows and orphans. Speak up for the oppressed. Submit to government. Use your gifts. Bear each other's burdens. Be thankful. Be joyful. Test everything, hold on to the good. Practice self-control. Resist temptation. Forgive again—and again, and again. Do justly. Love mercy. Walk humbly. Be gentle and respectful. Share the gospel.

Unlike your natural, deceptive, incurable, incomprehensible heart, these commands will never lead you astray.

THINK IT THROUGH, TALK IT OUT

1. How often do you hear the phrase "follow your heart"?

2. How do you feel about this advice after reading the chapter?

3. Tell about a time you followed your intuition and it steered you right. What about a time you followed your brain?

4. Kate says you should pay careful attention to the things that make you cry. What things make you cry? What things give you an excited, frantic energy? What things do you want to dive into headfirst?

5. What natural abilities do you have? How might those translate into a passion? What opportunities have you had the guts to say "yes" to?

6. What is a dream you would like to follow? What would you do if you were not afraid?

7. Kate said, "When you don't know what to do, just do what you know to do." What is something you know to do? What is a next right step for you—the next right thing?

CHAPTER

6

GET MAD, NOT MASTERED

"Emotions make good servants, but bad masters."
–Ellen Bowers

My favorite commentary on female emotion is from the movie *Sleepless in Seattle*. I realize that this movie came out when I was like, eight, which means you were probably not born yet. But I want to be Meg Ryan when I grow up—intelligent and spunky and classy and adorable. This movie is fantastic, and I bet your mom loves it—and if you offer to watch it with her, I bet she will buy you any pizza you want and maybe even new pajamas and make an evening of it. Just saying.

Anyway, there is this great scene where Rita Wilson melts down into blubbery hysterics recounting the plot of *An Affair to Remember*. She sniffles and chokes and fans her tears while the men in the room stare at her like she has three heads.

Then the men sarcastically break down into similar hysterics over *The Dirty Dozen*.

Sam Baldwin: I just want somebody I can have a decent conversation with over dinner. Without it falling down into weepy tears over some movie!

Greg: She's, as you just saw, very emotional.

Sam Baldwin: Although I cried at the end of *The Dirty Dozen*.[18]

Greg: Who didn't?

Sam Baldwin: Jim Brown was throwing these hand grenades down these airshafts. And Richard Jaeckel and Lee Marvin . . .

---

18. This is a WWII movie in which a lot of people get blown up. It came out almost TWENTY YEARS before I was born. Roughly the time of dinosaurs.

[Begins to cry]

Sam Baldwin: . . . were sitting on top of this armored personnel carrier, dressed up like Nazis . . .

Greg: *[Crying too]* Stop, stop!

Sam Baldwin: And Trini Lopez . . .

Greg: Yes, Trini Lopez!

Sam Baldwin: He busted his neck while they were parachuting down behind the Nazi lines . . .

Greg: Stop!

Sam Baldwin: *[Still crying]* And Richard Jaeckel—at the beginning he had on this shiny helmet . . .

Greg: *[Crying harder]* Please, no more. Oh! I loved that movie.

The premise in this silly and insightful scene is the same premise that the world is operating on, universally: girls are emotional. The scene is great because it holds up a mirror, and we see ourselves in all our hilarious humanness.

According to the media (and lunch table conversations everywhere), teen girls are so emotional that you burst into tears at the sight—nay, the thought—of your celebrity crush. Your emotional response is so exaggerated and insane that the term *fangirling* is a thing. And the emotional label follows you as you grow. As a woman, it's assumed that my big, bleeding heart dribbles all over the puppies I can't keep from rescuing, past the pile of overpriced school fund-raiser chocolate bars that I couldn't say no to, and over to the TV, where they soak my box sets of Hallmark Channel DVDs. (For me it's kittens, Thin Mints, and seasons of Grey's Anatomy. Potato, po-tah-to.) The presumption is that, as females, we have visceral, emotional reactions to breakups, weddings, and love songs, and that we literally lose control of our minds around babies. I can't object to any of this, as this year I've cried over commercials for the following:

The Olympics

Diet Coke

Pampers diapers

Publix grocery stores

Hallmark cards

Google Chrome

St. Jude's Children's Hospital

Although I maintain that—male or female, young or old—if you've never cried over a St. Jude's Children's Hospital commercial, you are a withered old stump without a heart. I mean, come on.

While I cannot object to the fact that women are emotional, I have major beef with the hyperbole—with the over-the-top jokes and jabs that pick at the "emotional woman" stereotype. It can be fun—but it's dangerous too.

The danger is in the nuance—the sneaky supposition that emotional reactions are unwarranted, out of place, or irrational. Hiding within every roll of the eyes, every humorous portrayal of a crazy, weepy girl, is the presumption that emotion is silly, weak, or lesser than stoicism. At the very best, those expressions of emotion are simply misplaced.

I reject this completely.

Do girls often react to things more emotionally than guys do? Sure. But a reaction is not the same thing as an *over*reaction.

Girls, if you accept the "overly-emotional" label, you'll subconsciously start to believe that your emotions are a liability and allow other people to treat you accordingly.

Here's what I see:

I see teachers, friends, coworkers, neighbors, bosses, pastors, and people all over every social media outlet dismissing the valid thoughts and valid opinions of girls under the banner of "she's just being emotional."

I hear girls apologizing for their feelings. "I'm sorry; I'm just a little emotional right now."

I see girls expressing legitimate concerns that are too often met with a patronizing pat on the back and a "There, there, it will all look better in the morning."

> DO GIRLS OFTEN REACT TO THINGS MORE EMOTIONALLY THAN GUYS DO? SURE. BUT A REACTION IS NOT THE SAME THING AS AN *OVER*REACTION.

In other words, I see girls getting dismissed and beat over the head with the "emotional card"—and I see girls taking it.

Enough is enough. In order to protect yourself from confusion, guilt, emotional abuse, and sexism, you need to recognize the false presumption that emotion is a liability—reject it—and embrace the truth found in God's Word.

In other words, stop taking it.

GOD IS EMOTIONAL

God created us—people—in His image. It's why some people are so endlessly creative and innovative, because God is The Creator, The Innovator. It's why some people are so brilliantly detail oriented, because they are reflections of a God who thought up organic chemistry and the quadratic equation and built an orderly universe. It's why every single one of us needs community, because He (as Father, Son, and Holy Spirit) exists for eternity in community.

Our emotions are reflections of the very heart of God.

God loves.

God hates.

God gets angry.

God feels regret.

God feels compassion.

God feels pity.

God feels grief and sadness.

God feels joy.

God feels longing.

God feels hurt.

God feels jealous.

God feels satisfaction and pride.

God feels delight.[19]

God *feels*.

And our God Who Feels placed within you a soul capable of strong, furious, overwhelming emotion.

Not just girls either. Guys are emotional beings because they too are created in the image of God. Some guys are more emotional than others, just like some girls are more emotional than others. Logically, then, it follows that there are some guys who are much more emotional than some girls. They are not mythical leprechaun-unicorn guys either; I actually know several.

As *humans*, we have the ability to be racked with sobs, to yearn and ache and howl inside. We can love so intensely that our chests leap and throb and ache. We can feel joy so deeply that the only sensation we can liken it to is flying. The point is, we feel things and our feelings move us—they affect us.

Our feelings are so instinctive that we sometimes get to be surprised by our own emotions. It's why we burst into spontaneous laughter, because we don't choose the joy as much as joy happens to us; it bubbles up from

---

19. See Jeremiah 31:3; Deuteronomy 12:31; John 2:13–15; Genesis 6:5–6; Matthew 9:36; Judges 2:18; John 11:35; Luke 15:4–6; Isaiah 30:18; Ephesians 4:30–31; Deuteronomy 4:23–24; Genesis 1:31; 2 Samuel 22:20.

somewhere deep inside. It's why we gasp, squeal, sigh, and moan—because those noises are as immediate as the emotions that prompt them; we utter them before we have the chance to attach words to what is happening inside of us.

God knitted us this way, and I believe that it gives Him great pleasure. God doesn't shun human emotion; He doesn't tell us to suck it up or to get over it. No, God *responds* to human emotion. His heart is moved by our desperation. The prodigal's shame and humility caused the father to run to him. Hannah's emptiness and sorrow prompted God to give her a son. The bleeding woman's hopelessness and desperation moved Jesus to heal her. The Israelites contrition caused God to restore them—over and over again. Gideon's fear caused God to affirm and encourage him. God rewarded King David's joyous, flamboyant, get-your-groove-on worship, and punished Michal for her snooty disapproval. Throughout history God is not only emoting, but responding to His people's emotions with expressions of grace so divine that they could only come from a loving, feeling God.

God is emotional. Don't apologize for that which God placed inside of you as a reflection of His own divine character.

And think twice before blasting a friend for getting really emotional after a breakup (or after failing a test or after a fight with a friend). Go easy on yourself if that person is you. No matter how "her own fault" her (or your) predicament is, no matter how preventable, immature, foolish, or shortsighted—there is still a hurting person under there. *Treat her* like a hurting person. You can't tell someone to stop feeling something. You can tell them to stop dwelling on something, stop thinking untruths, but you can't tell them to stop feeling, no matter what. The emotion is not the enemy anyway—the behavior is. Emotion is given to us as a gift from The God Who Feels. Respect it as such.

EMOTION IS GOOD

To say that emotion is good is so obvious, so undeniable and unavoidable, I don't know how anyone could argue it. Without emotion we are shells of people, lower than animals; we are robots. Life and literature are bursting with stories about how—all terror, pain, and sadness considered—it is better to feel than not.

In John 10:10 Jesus says that He came to give us life more abundant—and abundant it is. The life of a follower of Christ is a roller coaster filled to the brim with high highs and low lows. God gives us huge burdens, entrusts to us huge hurts, and requires of us huge sacrifices. He also lavishes joy, peace, and love without measure. Life with Christ is full.

Because we were created to live this full life, nothing less will do. This is one reason that men and women walk away from emotionless marriages. It's why emotionless friendships have short expiration dates. Our souls are meant to be intertwined with the souls of the people around us, tied together with love, trust, hurt, and forgiveness—doubled laughter and shared grief.

> GOD GIVES US HUGE BURDENS, ENTRUSTS TO US HUGE HURTS, AND REQUIRES OF US HUGE SACRIFICES.

Because we have emotional souls created to live emotional lives, every single relationship, from lovers to fellow humans in the grocery store, benefits equally, though differently, from our ability to engage emotion.

EMOTIONAL INTELLIGENCE

Every year, leaders in the science, health, and business industries say louder and clearer that a person's ability to recognize and use emotions makes them more efficient, more likeable, and—bottom line—a cut above the rest. The "emotion in business" ball really got rolling in 1990 when two professors coined the term "Emotional Intelligence." These two guys, Jack Mayer and Peter Salovey, define emotional intelligence as, "the subset of social intelligence that involves the ability to monitor one's own and others' feelings and emotions, to discriminate among them and to use this information to guide one's thinking and actions."

Okay, whoa. That's just a fancy way to say that, when we engage our emotions, it makes us smarter. (Which flies in the face of the myth that emotion sits opposite of reason and is nothing but a liability in decision making.) The ability to recognize and process what we are feeling makes us less socially awkward, boosts our people skills, makes us better leaders, bosses, and coworkers, helps us identify problems, and helps us resolve conflict gracefully.

Studies continue to reveal the same thing: the best, most successful, healthiest leaders have high emotional intelligence. People with high emotional intelligence are more likely to get promoted, and less likely to feel stressed. It's funny, isn't it? When science and experience and common sense start to tell us what God has been saying all along? All truth is God's truth, and the importance of emotion is a glittering example of it.

> PeoPle WitH HiGH emotional intelliGence are more likely to Get Promoted, and less likely to Feel StreSSeD.

Here are the four ways that emotional intelligence can work for you, like, today:

1. The ability to recognize your own emotions. *"I recognize that I am feeling defensive and edgy after the fight with my mom this morning."*

2. The ability to adjust your behavior based on the emotion you're experiencing. *"I am going to take a deep breath, shift my focus, and determine to have a positive, happy day at school."* Without the ability to recognize and respond to your emotion, you'd spend the day tense and snappy, which would affect your schoolwork and probably your relationships with friends, teachers, and coaches—all because you didn't have the wherewithal to intentionally shift your focus on the way to school; the fight and ensuing emotions would have controlled your whole day.

3. The ability to recognize emotions in other people. *"I can tell by her tone and her body language that my teacher is tired and annoyed."*

4. The ability to respond to other people based on the emotions that they are experiencing. *"I am not going to ask my teacher for an extra credit opportunity today. I'll wait until she's in a better mood."*

Don't listen to people who tell you to suppress, defy, or ignore your emotions. If you do, you'll lose an incredible tool that God gave you to help you navigate life. Emotion makes you smarter, not dumber.

EMOTION IS VALID

You're going to love this. In addition to being good, smart, and of God, your emotions are *valid*. No matter what they are, they're legit.

I am absolutely *over* seeing rational reactions labeled "melodramatic" just because they are emotional. I am tired of hearing condescending statements like, "Chill out," "Don't get all emotional," and "You're not thinking straight" directed at frustrated girls when frustration is the appropriate response.

Sometimes the right response is an emotional one.

Take grief, for example. Grief is one of the most profoundly necessary emotions; it must be acknowledged. There is no stiff-arming grief; it eats people alive when it's ignored; it steals souls. There is no way over, under, or around. At one point or another, all of us will have to march straight through it. As girls living in a fallen world, we are required to feel the full weight of hurt and loss. Grief is thick, tangible, and real. Grief isn't logical; it's emotional, and it's valid.

> Sometimes the right response is an emotional one.

Anger can be valid. Jesus taught me that. He shows us that it can be righteous, even. The sex-trafficking industry should make you angry. It should make you angry that the average age at which girls become victims of prostitution is twelve to fourteen years old. It should make you angry that roughly five thousand girls are trafficked and raped for profit every year in Atlanta alone. It should make you angry that babies are aborted just because they have Down syndrome; that should make your blood boil. The various racisms that Middle Eastern people, Hispanic people, and black people still feel in America should make you angry. Leymah Gbowee, Nobel Peace Prize winner, peace activist, and the President of Liberia, said it beautifully: "It's time for women to stop being politely angry." Right!? Don't try so hard to be dainty and peaceable and demure that you're afraid to feel things.

> Don't try so hard to be dainty and peaceable and demure that you're afraid to feel things.

Hurt is valid. So many things call for tears, girls. Betrayal, broken trust, offense, conviction, and compassion—they all make us cry and that's so, so good. One of the things I like best about my dad is that he's a cry-er. He hunts and fishes and smokes cigars and builds things, but he cries when he reads great poems or hears great music or tells me how much he loves me. He is strong and masculine and awesome, and he cries. And you can be strong and feminine and awesome, and cry. I love what Tina Fey wrote about being a boss and crying at work. In her book, *Bossypants*, she writes, "Some people say, 'Never let them see you cry.' I say, if you're so mad you could just cry, then cry. It terrifies everyone." When you are broken or moved—tears are good. It means you are alive. It means you can reckon with your feelings. When you feel compassion, tears are beautiful. You're not crying because you're hyper-emotional, you're crying because you're appropriately emotional.

Tears (lots and lots of tears) are a valid response to gratitude and grace. As long as I live, I will never forget one night in July 2007. I was engaged to the man who would become my husband, and he'd just found out that I'd made a terrible judgment. It was an enormous breach of trust, a selfish, thoughtless action that cut my good, good fiancé to the quick. And do you know what he did?

> tears (lots and lots of tears) are a valid response to gratitude and grace.

In the wake of the consequences of my own stupid decision, he stood up for me. He defended me, he forgave me, and he held me. In that moment, my fiancé was grace to me—and I wept. I crumpled up into the arms of the man I couldn't believe was still holding me, and I cried because I loved him so much. My tears were made up of some combination of brokenness, gratitude, disbelief, love, humiliation, and relief—and believe me when I say that every single tear was warranted. As my friend, Jamie, says, "There is not one single thing that is more life-changing than being on the receiving end of grace."

In the same vein, an emotional response to the gospel is a valid response. It's like the way my husband was grace to me, only times a million billion. When you think about how your sins have grieved the heart of God, when you think about the cross and what it cost Him, when you think about the reality of hell, the preciousness of your salvation, when you think about the certainty of where you'd be without the pursuing, enduring, unconditional love of Christ—it should move you. You should *feel something*. If you can think about your Creator sustaining you, carrying you, and remaining faithful to His every promise without regard to your adulterous heart and not be moved emotionally, I submit that you've never really encountered God. There is no way for a person to understand the severity of their sin and the matchless love of God without responding emotionally. It's the only response that makes any sense. It should flatten you.

ON BEING MASTERED

If you can muster the guts it takes to honor your emotions, you'll free yourself from so much future guilt and shame. Plus you'll be less likely to allow yourself to be dismissed in the workplace or emotionally abused in a relationship. It will change your life. But here's the deal: if you don't *also* muster the guts to stand up to your own emotions, you will become a monster. A sullen, pouty, entitled, mood-swinging, man-eating, fit-throwing, drive-all-your-friends-to-the-brink-of-insanity-and-back MONSTER. Gross.

Newsflash Emotions come naturally to you, dear teenage girl.

I bet that, so far, you are really tracking with me on this emotion thing. "I have THE RIGHT to be mad!" "It's okay to cry!" "God made me emotional!" "Emotions make me smart!" It's like I filled up your back-talk ammunition tank. The next time your parents tell you to chill out about something, you're going to open fire like, "Mom, if Jesus' BFF did what Sally just did to me He'd be mad too! Imma 'bout to cry and I'M NOT EVEN SORRY ABOUT IT." It's nice not to have to suppress or feel guilty about your emotions anymore.

However . . . learning not to act on every emotional impulse is a much harder pill to swallow—especially considering all of the drama and "follow your heart" nonsense that's been swirling around in your brain these last few years.

In 1 Corinthians 6:12 Paul writes one of my favorite declarations in the entire Bible:

"I will not be mastered by anything."

Paul is so hardcore. I love him. Part of living the Christian life is to be mastered, governed, by the Holy Spirit alone. As in, the Holy Spirit of God is the deciding factor in every choice; He is evident in every habit; in Him you live and move and have your being. Paul's declaration should be our declaration too. "I will not be mastered by anything." I will not be mastered by my selfishness, by my lust, by my hunger, by my alcoholism, by my substance abuse, by my anger, by my own impulses. I will not be mastered by pride or bitterness or unforgiveness. I will not be mastered by my hormones, my circumstances, or my thought-life. **And I will not be mastered by my emotions.**

My emotions do not control me; Christ controls me.

You HAVE to be able to say,

I will not retaliate just because I feel hurt. I will show grace because Christ controls me.

I will not have sex just because I feel love. I will remain pure because Christ controls me.

I will not scream at my parents just because I feel misunderstood. I will show respect because Christ controls me.

I will not quit my job just because I feel tired. I will work hard because Christ controls me.

The ability to feel something and respond, instead of react, is the essence of maturity. My forever-favorite definition of maturity is this:

"Maturity is not a vague philosophical concept, but a trained ability to meet the demands of reality." (Dr. Ted Roberts)

I believe so much that we, collectively as a society, should go all AWANAS[20] on the sixth graders in our midst and make them memorize that gem. I think that I should be able to stop you, or any given teenager on the street and demand that you recite the definition of maturity for me, on the spot. Who do I need to speak with to make this happen?

You are only as mature as you are able to reckon with reality. In other words, "REALITY CHECK!" Even if the demands of reality seem unfair, you've still got to deal with them, because they are real. That's what reality means. "This is real. This is the way it is; deal with it. Respond appropriately." And a lot of the time, meeting the demands of reality means doing things you don't *feel like* doing.

---

20. You know, AWANAS. It's like Girl (and Boy) Scouts for Baptists. You get a vest and a leader, and you receive badges and like paraphernalia for memorizing verses of Scripture each week. As an adult I know it as "that Wednesday night program at which a classroom full of second-grade girls try to get me to sign off on their verses after I feed them every single word of their verse, like they are little starlets and I'm their director holding the script off-stage." "For God so . . . LINE! Oh yeah, *loved* the world that He . . . LINE! Oh yeah, He *gave* His . . . LINE! Oh yeah, His only *begotten* son that . . . LINE!" Mercy.

The inability to get emotions under control is what gives girls everywhere a bad name. A girl who lets her emotions run amok is a fiery train wreck waiting to happen.

Let me just lay this out for you: if you don't learn how to manage your emotions, people will stop trusting you. You will be the girl who cried wolf, who overreacted at every pass in order to get attention or sympathy or admiration or praise or whatever it is you were hungry for at the moment. No one will be able to tell the difference between when you're really hurting and when you're just whining. You'll lose the support system you need for when things get tough, because people will be hesitant to reach out and carry you.

> tHe inaBiliTY to Get emotions unDer control is WHat GiVeS GirlS everywHere a BaD name.

Your friends, boyfriends (future husband?) won't open up to you. They'll try to protect you from your own reactions; they'll keep things from you because they don't think you can handle it. You'll get too angry, too hurt, too sad, too overwhelmed. You'll miss out on meaningful relationships because your hyper-emotionalism will keep everyone at a distance.

Having and expressing emotions adds positively to every interaction (even professional ones). Being mastered by emotions torpedoes every interaction (even intimate ones).

Darling, if you are mastered by your emotions, you are in just as much bondage as a girl mastered by alcohol or cutting. It's a more socially acceptable vice, but if you don't learn how to get out, how to get control, the habits you form will be detrimental to your adult life, negatively impacting your relationships, your career, and ultimately your own happiness.

GETTING CONTROL

To get control of your emotions, you must continually check them against two things:

1. Truth

2. The Word of God

Emotions, while valid, must always be subject to truth. Just because you feel something doesn't mean it's true. CAN I GET AN AMEN? And also, a "thank God!"? Because I feel a lot of dumb things sometimes. Just because you feel unwanted doesn't mean you are. Just because you feel right doesn't mean you are. Just because you feel your life is over doesn't mean it is. Just because you feel like he's your future husband doesn't mean he is. Just because you feel fat, unworthy, unlovable, or insignificant doesn't mean you are.

Wrong emotions are still real; they are cruel that way. A hurt is a hurt is a hurt, no matter how it came to be. Feelings must be acknowledged—and, a lot of times, the appropriate acknowledgment is, "I am feeling this thing. It is not true, even though it feels true."

Your feelings do not equal the truth. They don't trump the truth, either.

If whatever you're feeling conflicts with the Word of God, the feeling is wrong. Period. You don't need to pray about it anymore. The Word of God is unparalleled in its authority, which makes things nice and simple. Not easy, but simple. You feel like God abandoned you? That's fine, and we can deal with that emotion. We can talk about why you feel that way and what to do about it. We can encourage you and be there for you, but you've got to know—IT'S NOT TRUE. It can't be. Because God never said your feelings were infallible; He said His Word was. So that's the hierarchy, the order of operations.

FREEDOM

What I really, really want—way down deep in my gut—is for you to be free. I want you to be free to feel great big emotions without having to apologize for them. I want you to cry until it feels like the anvil has been lifted off of your chest. I want you to laugh easily, to jump up and down when you get excited and never worry about whether or not it's nerdy. I want you to get mad about injustice and not have to be polite about it. I ache for you to ache. I want you to yearn and rejoice and fall in love with all sorts of things. I want you to feel stuff. I want you to be free to feel, and I want you to be free to un-feel. I don't want you to drown under all of that feeling; I don't want it to overwhelm you or paralyze you. I want you to be free in every way. Not mastered by anything.

I'm on that journey too. The journey toward freedom and maturity—we're all on it until the day we are perfected in Jesus. Here is how I'm fighting for my freedom:

I write down every emotional lie I feel, no matter how big or small. (This isn't something I did one afternoon. I invite you to start, one day—one emotion, somewhere lasting that you can add to as you grow.)

The first entry on my page says,

"I feel like nobody *really* knows me."

Down the side of your page it might say:

I feel alone.

I feel like nobody understands me.

I feel like if anyone knew me, they wouldn't like me.

I feel unwanted.

I feel like the ugly duckling.

I feel like I'll never be good enough for this teacher.

I feel like I'll never be good enough for my parents.

I feel like I hate her.

I feel like I need him; if he dumps me I don't know what I'll do.

I feel afraid of the future.

I feel intimidated by the college application process.

And on and on—we have such a large capacity for emotion.

Here's where it gets awesome: match each feeling with a truth that directly addresses it. It doesn't have to be a Bible verse, though most of mine are, just something you know to be real.

After several months of recognizing feelings, recording them, and searching God's Word, you're going to have a weapon. You will have learned to wield that double-edged sword that the writer of Hebrews references: The Word of God, living and active, perpetually relevant. Eventually, your list might look something like this:

I feel alone. "Be content with what you have, because God has said, 'Never will I leave you; never will I forsake you'" (Hebrews 13:5).

I feel like nobody understands me. "O LORD, you have searched me and you know me. You know when I sit and when I rise; you perceive my thoughts from afar. You discern my going out and my lying down; you are familiar with all my ways. Before a word is on my tongue you know it completely, O LORD" (Psalm 139:1–4).

I feel like if anyone knew me, they wouldn't like me.
"For you created my inmost being; you knit me together in
my mother's womb. I praise you because I am fearfully and
wonderfully made; your works are wonderful, I know that full
well" (Psalm 139:13–14). "But God demonstrates his own love
for us in this: While we were still sinners, Christ died for us"
(Romans 5:8).

I feel unwanted. "He brought me out into a spacious
place; he rescued me because he delighted in me" (2 Samuel
22:20). "The LORD your God is with you, he is mighty to save.
He will take great delight in you, he will quiet you with his love,
he will rejoice over you with singing" (Zephaniah 3:17).

I feel like the ugly duckling. "The king is enthralled by
your beauty; honor him, for he is your lord" (Psalm 45:11). "All
beautiful you are, my darling; there is no flaw in you" (Song
of Solomon 4:7). "Your beauty should not come from outward
adornment, such as braided hair and the wearing of gold
jewelry and fine clothes. Instead, it should be that of your inner
self, the unfading beauty of a gentle and quiet spirit, which is of
great worth in God's sight" (1 Peter 3:3–4).

**I feel like I'll never be good enough for this teacher.
I feel like I'll never be good enough for my parents.** "But
he said to me, 'My grace is sufficient for you, for my power
is made perfect in weakness.' Therefore I will boast all the
more gladly about my weaknesses, so that Christ's power may
rest on me" (2 Corinthians 12:9). "Am I now trying to win the
approval of men, or of God? Or am I trying to please men? If

I were still trying to please men, I would not be a servant of Christ" (Galatians 1:10). "Whatever you do, work at it with all your heart, as working for the Lord, not for men" (Colossians 3:23).

I feel like I hate her. "For our struggle is not against flesh and blood, but against the rulers, against the authorities, against the powers of this dark world and against the spiritual forces of evil in the heavenly realms" (Ephesians 6:12). "You have heard that it was said, 'Love your neighbor and hate your enemy.' But I tell you: Love your enemies and pray for those who persecute you" (Matthew 5:43–44).

I feel like I need him; if he dumps me I don't know what I'll do. "I am he, I am he who will sustain you. I have made you and I will carry you; I will sustain you and I will rescue you" (Isaiah 46:4). "The LORD appeared to us in the past, saying: 'I have loved you with an everlasting love; I have drawn you with loving-kindness'" (Jeremiah 31:3).

I feel afraid of the future. "'For I know the plans I have for you,' declares the LORD, 'plans to prosper you and not to harm you, plans to give you hope and a future'" (Jeremiah 29:11).

I feel intimidated by the college application process. "For God did not give us a spirit of timidity, but a spirit of power, of love and of self-discipline" (2 Timothy 1:7). "I can do everything through him who gives me strength" (Philippians 4:13).

Can you even imagine how your life would be revolutionized if you could combat your emotions with that kind of stuff? You would be brave! Steady! Sure! Brennan Manning wrote, "How glorious the splendor of the human heart that knows that it is loved." And God wrote, "The truth will set you free." Babe, if you can internalize the truths found in God's Word, you will be splendid and free.

My personal list has been a treasure to me. My list has given me wits when I had no wits about me. The Word of God centers us; it focuses us, and tells us the truth—it will tell you the truth. When your emotions are threatening to leech the sense and logic right out of you, when they feel oppressive and suffocating and like the only real thing in the world, the Word of God is a lifeline back to reality. A list like this gives you the ability to feel what you're feeling (to write it down, it's fair! It's real and it matters!) and then to submit those very real feelings to the very real truth.

> IF YOU CAN INTERNALIZE THE TRUTHS FOUND IN GOD'S WORD, YOU WILL BE SPLENDID AND FREE.

It will change your life, and it will change the world. An entire generation of strong, brave girls—freed from the bondage of insecurity, grounded in the power of God, driven by great, big feelings, armed with truth—you are a force to be reckoned with. You will change the world.

THINK IT THROUGH, TALK IT OUT

1. On a scale of 1–10, how "emotional" of a person are you? Do you wear your emotions on your sleeve, or are you more private about the things you feel?

2. Are you a cry-er?

3. Have you ever thought about God being joyful and happy? Which one of God's emotions surprises you the most?

4. Have you ever been embarrassed about your emotions before? Why?

5. Have you ever heard of emotional intelligence before? How would growing your emotional intelligence be helpful to you in your friendships? At school? At home with your family?

6. What emotions tend to "master you" the easiest? Anger? Depression? Jealousy?

7. Someone said that emotions are like waves; you can't stop them from coming, but you can choose which ones to ride. How can you learn to master your own emotions?

CHAPTER
7

SMOKING IS NOT COOL

"Tobacco kills one third of the young people who use it."[21]

Smoking is not cool.

---

21. See http://www.thetruthcom/facts/1-in-3.

CHAPTER
8

SIX CIRCLES

"Let us live so that when we come to die even the undertaker will be sorry." -Mark Twain

"Regard your good name as the richest jewel you can possibly be possessed of—for credit is like fire when once you have kindled it you may easily preserve it, but if you once extinguish it, you will find it an arduous task to rekindle it again. The way to a good reputation is to endeavor to be what you desire to appear." -Socrates

Listen: when you insist that you don't care what anybody thinks about you, you sound like a heroin addict insisting that she can "quit any time she wants." In other words, you sound ridiculous. The thing you claim not to need is the very thing that consumes you. There is no more trend-conscious, fashion-conscious, reputation-conscious, approval-seeking creature on the planet than a teenage girl. That's not a jab; it is a reality. There are entire industries that exist solely because you care what other people think. There is a litany of medical and psychological disorders that spring from a teenage girl's obsession with what other people think. Thousands of grown women are in therapy every day because they cared what their fathers thought of them—what their mothers, friends, and classmates thought. Not knocking it; I love therapy. I've lived in four different states and I've seen counselors in three of them.

Eighty percent of the decisions people make in day are made with the aim to be well-liked: hair, clothes, music, weekend plans, the jobs they apply for, the language they use, and the company they keep—for starters. You are no exception.

If you assume that just because you have no desire to infiltrate the "in crowd," that you don't care what people think about you—you're missing it. Popularity might not be your aim, but caring what people think isn't about popularity; it's about belonging. A girl who "hates cheerleaders" will usually go to great lengths to differentiate herself from cheerleaders, effectively proving that she does care about how she is perceived—she just wants to be perceived as different. Caring about what people think isn't just for the insecure and the wannabes. The desire to belong to any group or non-group—the desire to be associated or disassociated from anyone or anything—is to care what people think.

> caring What People think isn't about popularity; it's about Belonging.

What's more, independence, free-thought, and a little rebellion are cool in every social circle, no matter how mainstream or obscure. If a girl gets a reputation for caring what other people think, she's called desperate, insecure, shallow, or a mindless sheep. There is no scarlet letter in girl-dom as shameful as Caring What People Think. Except for maybe dating a friend's ex; that'll get you tarred and feathered. It is very important to you that you be perceived as the kind of girl who doesn't care what other people think. The irony.

Humans are natural image-guarders, and as a teen girl, you take image-guarding to a whole 'nother level. The list of things teen girls will compromise, or downright sacrifice, to feel like they belong is long and terrifying.

When you say, "I don't care what you think about me," it's never true. What you mean is, "I don't care what this particular person thinks," or "I don't care what you think about this issue" (your clothes, your boyfriend, whatever), or "You don't have all the facts about me, so your opinion is incorrect and irrelevant."

But you care what people think about *you*—about who you are and what you're worth. I know because we all do.

It isn't just you. It isn't just teens or just girls or just women. All of us would run the gamut of *Fear Factor*'s worst—without blinking—if we knew that, at the end, was belonging. We would say, "So you're telling me that there will be a community of people that enjoy each other and carry each other along? There will be no loneliness or insecurity? I will be appreciated, needed, and missed when I'm not there? I'll be understood—truly known, and still loved? I can be a part of something bigger than myself? I'll have a home, a niche? **Okay.** I'll walk across fire for that. I'll climb into that bathtub full of leeches—as long as there is a tribe of friends to pull me out on the other side, and care for me." Belonging is one of the most powerful motivators.

Caring what other people think is not born of weakness or insecurity; it is born of the need for relationship—and it is a need. God saw that it wasn't good for man to be alone, and your primal desires for love, affirmation, validation, and friendship are reflections of that truth. Those impulses are tells—soul cravings. Community is how you were created to live. Community is the way you experience the love of God, through His people. Caring what people think is not a character flaw. The degree to which you care what people think doesn't make you egocentric or even insecure; it makes you human.

> caring WHat otHer people tHinK is not Born oF weaKness or insecurity; it is Born oF tHe neeD For relationsHiP.

You and I are grown-up versions of toddlers in our Cinderella dresses; we still need a safe place to land. You are a pre-stressed-out grown-up; you need a support system, just like I do.

If some friend ever made you feel like an imposter because you cared what someone thought; if someone ever called you out on it or told you not to care—I'm sorry. I'll never tell you not to care. Caring what other people think of you isn't the form of mental slavery people make it out to be. It's not insincere, shallow, or selling out. There is a middle ground between obsession with popularity and total disregard for your reputation. You won't automatically lose sight of your "true self" just because you care.

There is no need to wear "I don't care" like a badge of honor. Not caring doesn't make you stronger than anybody else. Usually, it just makes you lonelier.

PERCENTAGES

I am terrible at higher math. Really, really atrocious. I hung with math through Algebra 1, and I was actually kind of awesome at geometry; I can rock a proof. But after geometry comes Algebra 2, and that's where it went downhill. I failed the very first test of my entire academic career when I had to graph parabolas (or paraboles, or hyperboles, or hyperbolas or WHATEVER THEY ARE CALLED). When I did, something inside my Type A, first-born, irrationally competitive, eager-to-please heart broke, and math was dead to me. It does not matter how many math majors try to explain it, I still maintain that there is absolutely no point in having imaginary numbers. If I'm going to be imagining things, I'd much rather imagine fanciful worlds from *Harry Potter* than a bunch of make-believe numbers. Lame.

One of the subjects in math that I'm especially bad at is percentages. Every time I see a problem having to do with ratios or interest rates, something in my brain short-circuits. There is a pop, fizzle, and a puff of smoke and everything from that point forward is 100 percent made up (made up answers are a kind of imaginary number I can get on board with). This makes me a great tipper at restaurants; one time my husband looked over my shoulder and said, "Kate, you're leaving a 40 percent tip." Whoops.

I'm going to give you the benefit of the doubt here. Maybe the reason teen girls are so hot or cold about what people think about them— obsessing over it or rejecting it altogether—is not because you are immature or in denial. MAYBE you are just bad at math, like me. Maybe the notion that some people's opinions should carry more weight than others is entirely too much percentage-math to bother with.

You need to understand that everything doesn't count 100 percent. It's not all or nothing. All opinions are not equal.

> YOU GET TO CHOOSE WHICH VOICES STICK AND WHICH VOICES FALL BY THE WAYSIDE.

When you figure out *whose* opinions to listen to and *when*, you are free. You're free because, suddenly, you are allowed to care. You're allowed to need friends, allowed to value a good name. You are allowed to listen to what's true, but you're also allowed to ignore what isn't. You get to choose which voices stick and which voices fall by the wayside. That is power and confidence and freedom.

There is a cast of recurring characters in your life: God, you, your parents, your friends, classmates, and strangers. The opinions of every single one of these recurring characters matters—they just don't matter the *same*.

Here is a simple breakdown.

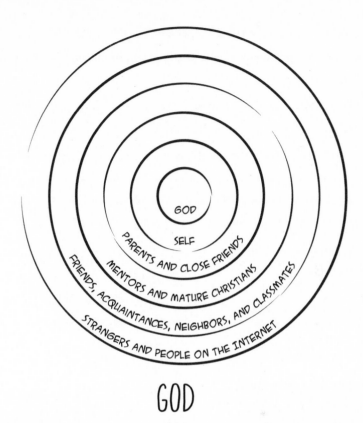

GOD

Bottom line: God is the only one operating with all of the information. When people form opinions about you, they do so by collecting clues from your appearance, your personality, your choices, the company you keep, and whatever other measure of popularity and worth that seems so important that week. Whether or not you have TOMS or just BOBS. Whether or not you've been kissed. It's craziness.

Only God knows every minute of every day you've ever lived (Hebrews 4:13).

Only God knows your innermost thoughts. (Psalm 139:1–4).

Only God knows every hurt, every motivation, every experience, big or small, that has shaped you in some way.

Only God is working with all the information (Romans 2:2).

In the Old Testament, God is called *El Roi*, "God who sees." Is that not the most glorious thing you've ever heard? God who sees. He sees me. He sees you. He sees us. At the end of your life, when you stand before God, you stand before the only One who has ever really known you.

Nobody else has the authority to say where you will spend eternity or why. No person, no matter how much they know, how loudly they speak, or how many people they influence, can add or detract a speck of value from your life—thank God. He has spoken, and He says you are the apple of His eye—end of discussion. On days you want to crawl under the covers and cry, you're enough. On days you've made huge, irreversible mistakes, you're enough.

> WHen you set out to Determine your WortH—WHen you consiDer How mucH you are loveD, anD How Deeply, GOD'S WorD is Final.

When you set out to determine your worth—when you consider how much you are loved, and how deeply, God's Word is final. If He says you need to be saved, you do. If He says you're sin-sick, you are. If He says you're forgiven, you are. If He says you're pure and lovely, you are.

In this supreme sense, God's opinion of you is the only one that matters.

SELF

Second only to God, you know more about yourself than anybody else does.

There are delicate dreams, secret desires, and injuries of heart that your parents don't know. No matter how tight you and your parents are, there is a lifetime worth of thoughts and feelings that they'll never know. Some you may have intentionally hidden, but mostly, there are just too many thoughts in a day; you couldn't share them all, even if you wanted to. It's a matter of sheer volume. Your life is littered with conversations, experiences, relationships, and lessons that will only ever be yours, privately. Such is personhood—so much happens to us when we are alive.

I love Rose's line from the movie *Titanic*, "A woman's heart is a deep ocean of secrets." What starts as a puddle of private feelings in childhood grows into an ocean by adolescence.

When you value the opinions of other people over what you know to be true, those false labels will wrap themselves around your heart like a hungry boa constrictor. They'll squeeze—gently, steadily—until they strangle your heart to death. Death by insecurity and frantic people-pleasing. Listen: you have my permission to believe the truth about yourself. First God's truth, and then your own—even when you are the only two who know it.

PARENTS

I promised to tell you the truth, so I'm just going to forge ahead even if you hate me for the next thirty seconds: the opinions of your parents carry more weight than the opinions of anyone in the outer rings of the circle for two reasons:

1. Parents know their kids.
2. You are under orders to honor them.

Bam.

Let me explain. Parents (or whichever family members you grew up with) have observed you, almost scientifically, from the moment of your births. They watched your personality come to life long before you could even talk. They know whether you are strong-willed or easy-going, what things motivate you, and what things scare you. They've spent years listening. Apart from God and yourself, the people who know you best are your parents.

You may beg to differ. You might believe that your friends know more about you because you tell your friends more than you tell their parents. That's true, and your friends may have more information, but parents have more *insight*. Friends know more, parents know deeper. Parents possess a breed of wisdom that only comes by experience—they earned it with age. Your dad might not know who you have a crush on this week, but he could pick you out of a crowded football stadium in two hot seconds by your gait. Your parents can spot tendencies and patterns in your life before you recognize them for yourself. They're not omniscient, but they're smarter than you think.

> your FrienDS May Have more inFormation, But ParentS Have more inSiGHt.

You are commanded to honor these parents that know you. Not just you—me too. This commandment does not expire when you turn eighteen. When you're young and living at home, honor means obey. When you become independent, honor does not *necessarily* mean obey, though it can. It *does* mean listen. It means respect, love, serve, consider greater than yourself, and submit to in love. As a grown woman, I can do things that my parents don't love, but to remain in good conscience (and right with God), I must honor them.

Girls, your mom birthed you, and it was gory. She fed you, and you bit her. She cleaned your own filth off of you for nearly a decade. She survived "the terrible twos" and only exposed you to a small bit of profanity when she couldn't strap the car seat into the car. She comforted more tantrums than she videotaped, and that earns her the right to speak to your actions and thoughts in a unique way. You must do more than *consider* her opinion, you must value it.

Note: I include mature Christians in this category too. They have the same wisdom born of age, and as brothers and sisters in Christ, they have the Word of God and the Holy Spirit as their guide. If a pastor or a mentor shares an opinion in love, you better listen up.

BEST FRIENDS

Your friends' opinions matter for one big, gigantic reason: friends matter.

Eventually, your best friend will misunderstand you—maybe even betray you. One day you'll be offended by her, and her by you.

Your friends will tell you that they hate your boyfriend; they just will. Every time. They may tell you that the college you chose is a waste of your time. They may tell you that you're being dumb, shallow, mean, selfish, jealous, dramatic, or any number of other things that you will be to your friends. My friends told me these and more. Sometimes they were right, and sometimes they weren't. Maybe your friends will be right, and maybe they won't, but their rightness is irrelevant.

You don't get to dismiss the opinions of your friends out of hand just because you disagree. That kind of close-mindedness and defensiveness is a quick way to kill a friendship.

There is a great, big, giant-squid-sized difference between caring what friends think and internalizing everything they say, and making choices to appease people (see Galatians 1:10). No one should live their lives at the mercy of the fickle, uninformed opinions of other people; that's insane. But you can't disregard them; that's unwise—and kind of a punk thing to do.

When you grow up, you're going to need someone who knows you—someone who knows all your stories. When you are twenty-five years old, you will need someone you can call at 11:00 at night because you're having the worst day. You will need someone who is committed enough to your friendship to buy a plane ticket to come visit—someone that hasn't just *heard* about your struggles but has walked through them with you. You will need someone who has loved you at your ugliest, forgiven you, and stuck around. We all need someone we can trust completely.

One of the most beautiful descriptions of a friend was written by Dinah Maria Craik when she said,

> Oh, the comfort, the inexpressible comfort of feeling safe
> with a person; having neither to weigh thoughts nor measure
> words, but to pour them all out, just as they are, chaff and
> grain together, knowing that a faithful hand will take and sift
> them, keep what is worth keeping, and then, with the breath of
> kindness, blow the rest away.[22]

It takes years, tears, compromise, and a lot of grace to build a friendship like this. It doesn't happen overnight, no matter how much a pair has in common. You will cripple yourself, make it impossible to build this kind of friendship, if you dismiss every hurtful opinion.

> YOU HAVE TO LEARN TO CARE ABOUT THINGS YOU WOULDN'T NORMALLY CARE ABOUT FOR THE SAKE OF ANOTHER PERSON.

You have to learn to care about things you wouldn't normally care about for the sake of another person. This is the essence of selflessness. It is evidence of maturity and necessary for friendship.

---

22. See http://www.geonius.com/eliot/quotes.html.

The opinions of friends don't determine your value (only God can do that), and they aren't the same thing as absolute truth, but they matter.

They matter because friends matter.

COMMUNITY

Your community is comprised of all the people you see on a regular basis: your classmates, teammates, neighbors, boys you have a crush on, people you babysit for, and Starbucks baristas. The impression that this eclectic group of people holds of you is known as your "reputation."

We need to get something straight. Reputation IS NOT synonymous with stereotype, rumor, or unfounded prejudgment. Reputation does not mean "stuff people make up, imagine, or presume about you." Reputation means "the things you are *known for.*"

If the consensus within your community is that you are a snob, it means that this great, varied assortment of people (Republicans, Democrats, old, young, Christians, atheists, and everyone in between) who disagree on virtually *everything other thing* can all agree that you are a snob.

MAJOR RED FLAG.

One person can misjudge you; a group of friends can misjudge you. But if you have a reputation—if you're known by your community as a snob? It either means that you are, or that whatever you're putting out there is making you appear to be.

It's like eye witnesses in a court case: If one person claims to have seen something, there's a chance they are mistaken. If ten people saw it, it's probably true. But if two hundred strangers standing on a crowded street all describe the exact same incident in perfect detail? Bang the gavel, case closed—book 'em.

> **Your community is on the witness stand, your behavior is the evidence, and the verdict is your reputation.**

Your community is on the witness stand, your behavior is the evidence, and the verdict is your reputation.

If you get a reputation for being snide (or a flake, or of not keeping your word), it matters. A bad reputation is an indictment on your character. It should matter to you if almost every person you come into contact with walks away from the interaction thinking you're snide. Either everyone is right—in which case you should make some major changes to your character; or everyone is wrong—in which case you should make some major changes to your behavior. Either way, you've got a problem on your hands.

The opinions of others cannot detract value from your life, but they can detract credibility, and credibility matters.

Reputation matters because:

1. You want friends to like you and trust you.
2. You want teachers to give you a break when you forget your homework.
3. You're going to have to meet a boyfriend's parents someday.
4. You're going to need a job someday.
5. One day you're going to need help moving furniture and nobody is going to volunteer their truck if they think you're an ungrateful snob.

Don't be so busy trying to be all highly-evolved and confident and fierce that you forget about your reputation. You can be perfectly self-assured and still be aware of the impression you leave on those around you.

"A good name is more desirable than great riches; to be esteemed is better than silver or gold" (Proverbs 22:1). If you live with integrity and grace, a good reputation will inevitably follow. If anyone ever says anything bad about you, your community will come to your defense: "Oh, you must have caught her on a bad day! Perhaps there was a misunderstanding. Maybe she was PMSing, or being sarcastic. That is not the girl we know." We should all endeavor to live in such a way that, if anyone were to speak ill of us, no one would believe them.

We should all endeavor to live in such a way that, if anyone were to speak ill of us, no one would believe them.

STRANGERS ON THE INTERNET

The opinions of strangers on the Internet carry the least weight of all. They know little to nothing about you, and what they do know is only what you choose to share. Presumptions from such people are shallow at best, and often baseless. You CANNOT live by the praise of strangers on the Internet—hits on a blog, likes on an image. It's a trap. Cornelius Lindsey said, "If you live off a man's compliments, you'll die of his criticism."

Here's what I learned when I started a blog: a lot of people don't like me—and almost all of them are on the Internet. No girl can police the Internet from her bedroom. You can't answer every objection or address every criticism. Internet critics are like gray hairs; you pick one off and three more show up in its place. You'd have an easier time wrangling a pig greased with butter than you would trying to explain and defend yourself to the Internet trollers; it's an uphill battle—and it's up the *wrong hill*. You must tell yourself, often, that they don't know anything. That they are picking fights, flinging insults, hiding in the Internet, and that those ill-informed words are not worth the energy it takes to dwell on for one more minute. You can't make them like you, so just whatever about them. What you *can* do is behave in a way that reflects your nature, a way that is becoming to a follower of Jesus.

While strangers don't have much authority to talk about the issues in your life, the way *you* present yourself *to them* still matters. It matters because God says it does.

"By this all men will know that you are my disciples, if you love one another." (John 13:35)

"In the same way, let your light shine before men, that they may see your good deeds and praise your Father in heaven." (Matthew 5:16)

Do this with gentleness and respect, keeping a clear conscience, so that those who speak maliciously against your good behavior in Christ may be ashamed of their slander. (1 Peter 3:16)

"A good tree cannot bear bad fruit, and a bad tree cannot bear good fruit. . . . Thus by their fruit you will recognize them." (Matthew 7:18, 20)

The fruit of the Spirit is love, joy, peace, patience, kindness, goodness, faithfulness, gentleness and self-control. (Galatians 5:22–23)

These biblical mandates don't jibe with "I don't care what anybody else thinks of me."

As Christians, our job is to point others—everyone, strangers—to Christ. We are to be known as loving people, givers, and forgivers. We should be noticeably full of joy, patience, kindness, gentleness, and self-control—proof that the Holy Spirit is real and living and governing our lives.

I'm sorry that our society is guilty of selling you half-truths wrapped up as encouragement and pithy advice. "It doesn't matter what other people think about you," is not true. It's half true. And as author K. P. Yohannan wrote, "The trouble with half-truths is that they contain within them full lies."

> **We are to be known as loving people, givers, and forgivers.**

I know you can hardly wait to reject the expectations and judgments placed on you by an unforgiving society. You refuse to sacrifice your rights as a free citizen just because someone somewhere doesn't approve! You are leading the charge to free everyone from social slavery! At least that's what you think you're doing, based on all the pithy half-truth-lines we keep feeding you. But the reality is less kicking-tails-and-taking-names and more stupidly-shooting-yourself-in-the-foot.

Relationships matter, reputations matter, testimonies matter. You should care what other people think about you.

CHRONIC OVERCORRECTORS

History repeats itself. We are always discovering a new way of doing things that is really an old way of doing things. In style: bangs are in; no, they're out; no, they're hot. Skinny jeans are in; no, they're gross; no, they're rockstar. In parenting: babies should sleep on their stomachs; no, their backs; no, their stomachs. In nutrition: butter is healthier; no, margarine is healthier; no, it's definitely butter. In religion: we should focus on discipleship; no, evangelism; no, discipleship.

We humans are chronic overcorrectors. We swing wide one way, then the other—each generation trying to compensate for the weaknesses of our parents, each revealing weaknesses of our own. Back and forth, back and forth, through the ages.

C. S. Lewis used to say that for every current book he read, he'd read a really old book. The reason, he said, was that we are prone to chronological prejudices. As in, "It's newer, therefore it is more relevant. The way we do things now is better, smarter, and more efficient than the way our parents (and grandparents) did things."

I think about this a lot at church when I hear things like "This is not your grandparents' church." "We aren't afraid to be real." "We believe in engaging the culture." "We believe in community and doing life together." As if my generation invented authenticity. Like all the Christians who came before us for hundreds of years loved hypocrisy and judgment and nobody before us ever thought of using the New Testament church as a model.

Every time I consider our world, Scripture proves itself right again: there is nothing new under the sun.

A few generations ago, the advice, "Your reputation matters; you should care what people think of you" hardly needed to be said. People would have looked at you and said, "Duh," because that is the kind of thing people said a few generations ago. At the time, people lived in smaller, more rural communities. The Internet didn't exist. Verbal agreements were binding; your word was your bond; you shook on things.

But when we are left to our own devices, we take things too far. I'm sure it started with a few overachieving Type A personalities who were all, "I'm going to *win* at caring what people think!" What started out as building a good name within a community (which is wise), devolved into finding self-worth in what others thought (which is damaging)—and everything got all messed up.

People became chronic people-pleasers.

They were afraid to say "no."

All criticism felt like a personal attack.

People felt overwhelming pressure to conform.

People put as much stock in a stranger's opinion of them as they did in what they knew to be true of themselves.

An entire generation of young women spent their best years haunted by the words, "But what will people *think*?" As they matured, they saw the unnecessary burden they'd been carrying around all those years; they understood that the obsession with what other people thought was the root of their crippling insecurity and shame. So they vowed never to place that same burden on their daughters. They whispered to their little girls as they tucked them in at night, "It doesn't matter what anybody else thinks about you; you are beautiful." They comforted them through middle school rumors and high school drama, "It doesn't matter what anybody else thinks about you; you know what's true." And they said proudly at graduation celebrations, "Don't dwell on what everyone else thinks; you can accomplish anything you set your mind to."

It is no surprise that the next generation of young women held high the banner of "It doesn't matter what anybody thinks about me!" Their parents weren't crazy; the ability to weed out unhelpful opinions is healthy. It is essential to realizing our worth. It is helpful in doing what's right, even when it's not popular—for standing up for what we believe in. It is crucial in order to foster any kind of creativity. But in our zeal we take it too far. The girls who were taught not to care what people thought about them overcorrected and are living with a set of consequences they never saw coming. Do you see yourself in these? Can you foresee it, if you keep thinking and acting the way you are right now?

They sacrificed their relationships with their parents because they didn't care what they thought.

They uncensored themselves. They voiced rude and gossipy remarks under the guise of "I don't care what anyone thinks; I'm just telling *the truth*."

They became increasingly egocentric. Their own opinions were the only standard for their behavior.

They dismissed advice (and often common sense) because there was no reason to listen; it only mattered what they thought anyway. Outside opinions about their choices were uninformed and therefore irrelevant.

Friendships ended unnecessarily because they chose being "true to themselves" over reconciliation and compromise. They became islands unto themselves, worshipping independence and personal conviction.

In short, they are lonely. Also, they might have an ill-advised Tweety Bird tattoo (as ALL Tweety Bird tattoos are) because "What do my parents know? Of course I won't regret it. I can make adult decisions on my own!" The irony of Tweety Bird tattoos representing mature adult decisions is not lost on me.

Adolescence is the season of boundary-pushing. It's "the terrible twos," round two. It is self-discovery and unfurling tiny wings and leaping out of nests. You are especially susceptible to the lure of "I don't care what anybody thinks of me" because it suits you. It is the perfect sentiment on which to build any argument. If your mom objects to the clothes you want to wear, your friends, or the things you do on the Internet, all you have to do is proclaim, "But it doesn't matter what anyone else thinks about me!"

It's great because, if your parents have been feeding you that line for a while now, they'll have nowhere to go from there. Anything they say will be a contradiction of themselves, so they'll just stand there, floundering, mouths agape—like a trout.

Our culture has been using the phrase "It doesn't matter what anybody else thinks about you" to instill self-confidence for so long that you've started using it to make your crazy choices sound noble instead of completely ridiculous.

"I'm going to get this face tattoo and if my boss has a problem with it, then she's shallow and cares too much about appearances." Um, no.

"If Suzy thinks I'm a snob, then she doesn't have to hang out with me anymore, nobody's forcing her. I know I'm a nice person and that's what matters." I hope you like being alone.

"I'm going to take the job at Hooters even though my parents don't want me to. I need a job and don't care what anyone thinks about me." LORD, HAVE MERCY.

As idealistic as it may sound, that kind of reasoning is short-sighted, self-centered, and immature.

Remember maturity? It is not "a vague philosophical concept, but a trained ability to meet the demands of reality." Welcome to the real world, kiddos. Put on your big-girl pants and repeat after me:

Not getting a face tattoo isn't conformist; it's mature.

Caring what Suzy thinks (and honoring her thoughts and preferences over your own for the sake of a friendship) isn't weak; it's mature.

Being nice to someone you don't like isn't hypocritical; it's mature.

Keeping your mouth shut isn't cowardly; it's mature.

Accepting criticism and using it to grow isn't letting other people define you; it's being mature.

I have no doubt that some sweet, precious girls will take the advice "Your reputation matters; you should care what others think of you" too far. They'll swing wide like so many generations before them and run themselves ragged, threadbare, trying to get everybody to like them. They'll make themselves crazy thinking about it, and that will be a tragedy.

We're overcorrectors. We are kids on a balance beam, just trying to get from one side of life to the other, uninjured and unembarrassed. We wobble one way, then the other, trying to find a balance that's sustainable—a way of living that will get us to the other side without all the violent back and forth. No whiplash and no regrets: that's the goal.

> WE ARE KIDS ON A BALANCE BEAM, JUST TRYING TO GET FROM ONE SIDE OF LIFE TO THE OTHER, UNINJURED AND UNEMBARRASSED.

I believe the balance is grace.

Grace for ourselves. What others think doesn't define me.

Grace for others. Their opinions are valid; I'll listen graciously.

Grace for everyone.

There is no other way.

THINK IT THROUGH, TALK IT OUT

1. Whose (human) opinion of you is the most precious to you? Whose approval would be meaningful and encouraging to you? Why?

2. Why do we care so much about what other people think? Why does Kate say that caring what other people think isn't a sign of weakness or insecurity?

3. What do you think of when you hear the word "belonging"? What do you feel?

4. What is the difference between taking care of your "good name" and living based on other people's opinions?

5. Why is it so damaging to live trying to please everybody?

6. Why does your reputation matter?

7. Personally, should you start caring a little more what other people think about you? Or a little less?

CHAPTER 9

DUMB IS NEVER CUTE

"Above all, be the heroine of your own life, not the victim." -Nora Ephron

"You are a woman with a brain and reasonable ability. Stop whining and find something to do." -Lady Grantham, Downton Abbey

"We have to declare a princess-free zone. No tiaras, no Girls Gone Wild, no pretending we can't carry things. No fairytales, no waiting around to be rescued, and absolutely no playing dumb." -Shauna Niequist

Women have come a long way.

If you had been born in the Jianxgi province of China in the year 2000, there's a good chance you would have been aborted when your parents discovered you were a girl. If you'd been born in India, it's not likely that you would have been taught to read or write. If you'd been born in Saudi Arabia, you would need permission from your male guardian to travel or receive an education. If you'd been born in the Democratic Republic of Congo, you would have a 22 percent chance of being sexually abused. If you'd been born in the United States before 1920, you would not have been able to vote, because at the time a woman's opinion on matters of country was irrelevant. Until the 19th amendment was ratified, 50 percent of the population was muted, politically speaking, because of our gender and its implicit roles.

Indeed, women, across all cultures, have come a very long way.

Even so, female CEOs and Supreme Court justices, like Facebook's Sheryl Sandburg and Justice Ruth Bader Ginsburg, are still overcoming prejudices that peg women as overly-emotional, indecisive, and only passable at math, mechanical, and leadership skills. These women at the top of their fields are fighting hard, even now, to demonstrate that women are not ruled by their sympathies (or their hormones), that they can be an integral part of any team, and that they can lead well.

You would do well to remember the world into which you were born a girl, and to remember the worlds into which you, mercifully, were not. Thanks to the tenacity of women that have gone before, you are as likely, if not more likely, to be accepted into college as your male counterparts. Female leaders exist in virtually every field. There are female surgeons, film directors, lawyers, executives, comedians, entrepreneurs, astronauts, pilots, and professional athletes. Growing up, you believed that you could be anything—and your generation is one of the first that could dare to think so.

The world is vast and big and bright for you. Nearly limitless—and too many women have worked too hard to see women esteemed for you to act like a flirtatious twit to get what you want.

> too many women have worked too hard to see women esteemed for you to act like a flirtatious twit to get what you want.

THE PRICE

Girls, this is a "put on your big-girl pants" moment. I am appealing to you on behalf of ALL WOMEN. We are on the same team, you and me. Team ovaries. Team X chromosome. I am asking you to think about your life as it is now: the way boys treat you, the way grown men treat you. I'm also asking you to think about your future: the job you want to have, the things you want to accomplish, the way you want to be heard and loved. This is what's up:

There is a double standard in the minds of too many girls that goes something like this: If a guy manipulates you—if he romances you to get what he wants (for you to do his homework, or whatever else)—he's a pig. But if you manipulate a guy, you were just using your feminine wiles, a tool in your arsenal, to get what was coming to you.

I'm surprised by how many grown women believe that the flippant manipulation of men is within the parameters of womanhood. Like, we're girls so if we're devious, it's not really devious, it's just sexy or sly or something.

If you cite PMS to get out of gym, even when PMS, for you, isn't excruciating cramps, but just an average amount of yuckiness—I'M LOOKING AT YOU, BABE. If you've ever seriously considered using your cleavage to get out of a speeding ticket, if you flirt to procure information, or if you exaggerate your princess-y frailness to get guys to do all your heavy lifting—wake up. I hear women banter with each other sometimes, saying things like, "I can get whatever I want from my boyfriend," or "I'm not ashamed that I flirt to get favors—I can!" They're laughing, but they're not joking, and I want to grab them by the shoulders and shake them and say, "YOU ARE GIVING GIRLS EVERYWHERE A BAD NAME!"

I suppose I get it; I get that control makes you feel powerful—and empowerment is like a Starbucks blueberry scone: once you have it you wonder how you ever lived without it, and there is absolutely no turning back. I understand that eliciting a desired response from a guy makes you feel beautiful and unstoppable and wanted—the very things that the guys you care the most deeply about don't make you feel often enough. The whole thing is very practical. It works, as long as the ends justify the means.

But I want to call attention to the logical end of this thinking. Whether you are manipulating out of a place of entitlement or of pure practicality, you are manipulating to your own detriment.

It'll be hard for you to insist that PMS doesn't handicap your decision making or your emotional stability if you've been using it to justify every lazy impulse and emotional lashing out since the sixth grade. So suck it up; your grown-up self will thank you.

Just think: a woman can't flirt her way to the top and then be surprised when someone accuses her of not having the chops to do the job. She can't be offended at the insinuation that she doesn't have the work ethic if she's never ACTUALLY SHOWN ANYONE HER WORK ETHIC. "Work ethic" is not synonymous with "coy conversational undertones." They both work, but they aren't the same, so don't expect the outcomes to be.

This kind of behavior is a bait and switch; it's like saying, "Look at how fabulous my lips are! Look how pouty and enticing. I am laughing at all of your jokes with my perfectly-glossed lips that, by now, you are thinking about kissing. You should keep me around and happy so that I will keep pouting my flirty lips at you." And then, in the very next breath saying, "How dare you say that I only got this job because of my lips!?"

This kind of stunt is how chicks get reputations as snakes. It doesn't mean girls aren't qualified, but how could anyone possibly know? Girls, you either show the world that you have brains, passions, and skills—or you don't. You can't have it both ways.

> YOU either SHOW the world that YOU Have Brains, Passions, and Skills—or YOU Don't. YOU can't Have it Both ways.

Of course you can bat your eyelashes, show a little skin, and giggle your way into a job, into a man's heart, or into the spotlight. You're adorable. But at what cost?

The cost of being an ego-stroker first and a talent second—once you get there—is inadvertently communicating that it's okay to manipulate other people. The cost is inadvertently communicating that ego-stroking is what girls have to do to be successful, or at least, it's what you had to do. The elite group of people who have risked life and limb to climb Mount Everest aren't impressed by someone who helicopters to the top.

> once you Start Batting eyelashes, eyelashes is all you've Got.

It's not where you are that counts; it's how you get there. If you don't have standards on the way up, you can't claim to have them once you arrive—wherever it is you're going. You won't lose your skill, but you will lose your credibility. Once you start batting eyelashes, eyelashes is all you've got.

That price is too high. My own credibility, the esteem of women and the way we think and work, is not something I'm willing to sacrifice on the altar of "but it's so fun!"

If you believe that suggestive flirting and damsel-in-distress-ing is just a way to level the playing field, you gravely underestimate yourself and the strength and intelligence of the female race. The only thing required to level the playing field is for you to march into the arena and break out the big guns: passion, skill, education, and well-reasoned opinions.

You are not a twit, so don't act like one because you think it serves you. It's a short-term perk with an ugly underbelly; it's a trap. It's easy to feel like you've won when you can flirt and seduce and get whatever you want—until you realize you've been objectified or patronized. Then it doesn't feel much like winning anymore. No matter what you get in the end (fame, fortune, a promotion at work, the guy of your dreams, or a discount at the mechanic), if you've been objectified along the way, it's not a win. It's a big, fat loss for present-you, for future-you, for women everywhere.

> You are not a twit, so don't act like one because you think it serves you. it's a short—term perk with an ugly underbelly.

THE RICHARD SIMMONS OF PRAYER: ON LIVING AT POINT M

Femininity is a superpower, not a one-trick pony. I want you to work your femininity in all of its glorious whole-ness, not prostitute it, offering your body up for enjoyment (physically or mentally) in exchange for something you want. If you think this is just the way the world works, you may be right—but we've got to change that. We've got to start living our ideals instead of our practicalities.

When I was in high school, I went on a mission trip every summer to Tijuana, Mexico, and San Diego, California. Our team ran Vacation Bible Schools to support churches and orphanages in Mexico, and we attended an apologetics and evangelism conference in California. As a part of the conference, each student was to spend a day in prayer and fasting. There was a contingent of students that stayed on campus each day to be guided in prayer by one of the conference leaders named Paul. Five minutes into my day of prayer I knew—this was an experience that I had no category for. My comfort zone was obliterated. Paul was expressive and uninhibited. There was lots of singing and shouting and crying out, lots of clapping and extending of arms. Paul used language I'd only heard in televangelist sermons. Halfway through the day we went on a prayer walk, and while we were en route, my friend leaned in and whispered to me, "Kate, he's like the Richard Simmons of Prayer!"

Listen, if you don't know who Richard Simmons is, stop right now, get online, and find a picture of that crazy man. No—a video. I am here to tell you that you can pray and laugh at the same time, because I did—for the next six hours. I think at one point Paul may have shouted, "I'm a pony! I'm pony!" When we debriefed with our team at the end of the day, I told my youth pastor's wife about my experience. She laughed with me, then told me something I've never forgotten. She said, "Sometimes we need someone down at Point M to help us move from Point A to Point B."

The Richard Simmons of Prayer changed the way I pray. He taught me that I could fast and pray all day and never grow bored. Weary, but never bored. He taught me about living in constant communication with God, about how to approach the throne boldly in my time of need, about how reverence looks, and about how to listen—how to speak *with* God, not just at Him. My expression in worship and prayer changed because of The Richard Simmons of Prayer; I began to understand how inextricably the physical is connected to the spiritual. I moved from A to B.

That is what it means to take a stand—to be an advocate. You live at Point M (and probably get labeled excessive and fanatical) to draw people toward the truth you believe in, a truth so big it's worth standing for. Advocates obliterate comfort zones, moving everyone around them from A to B.

I am willing to live down at Point M for you. YOU'RE WELCOME. I am willing to adopt a zero-tolerance policy against flirting for gain. Why are we so afraid to do this—the absolutely-zero-fake-twitty-manipulative-flirting thing, I mean? It's not unrealistic and it won't make us cold; it will make us sincere. You have nothing to lose unless the whole of your feminine charm is found in your ability to play princess. I don't understand the hesitation; are guys afraid that no one will want to flirt with them sincerely? Are girls so cold that, if we were to get rid of empty flattery, we'd have nothing left to praise? Speak the truth in love; encourage each other while the day is called today; kind words are like honey, sweet to the soul and health to the body—these are the truths of Jesus. So be a light! Encourage others liberally, be generous with praise; pile and dump and schmear it on. Be warm and charming and sincere. Love people well—and know that in so doing, there is no room for manipulation.

I believe that girls manipulating boys (by flirtation or any other means) isn't as innocent as our culture suggests. I believe that it is damaging to the cause of girls. What's more, I believe that, gender issues aside, people manipulating other people is never okay. Girls, dumb is never cute.

Don't be a twit; be better than that. Don't undermine yourself and, for crying out loud, don't undermine me. I'm advocating for you, and I

> love people well—and know that in so doing, there is no room for manipulation.

want you to join me. Adopt a zero-tolerance policy for twit-dom; do it for yourself and for girls everywhere. We are *all* on the same team. I look into the face of my darling five-year-old Madeline, who asks me questions about her small intestine and Neptune and atoms and the omnipresence of God, my girl who is socially skilled and exceptionally nurturing, and I know I must carry the torch that has been passed to me by the women who've gone before: the women who did hard things—who maybe didn't achieve everything they could have if they'd flirted a little more, but by taking a stand, achieved even more.

I am calling for you and your friends and your mamas and your grandmamas to carry their torches too.

> i am calling for Beautiful, Gentle, compassionate Girls— With Spines and Wills of Steel.

I am calling for strong girls. Not androgynous girls. Not harsh, shrill, or prudish girls. I'm calling for beautiful, gentle, compassionate girls—with spines and wills of steel. I'm calling for girls who know their value, their intelligence, and their skill, and behave accordingly.

HOW NOT TO BE A TWIT

Here are nine ways for you to make sure you're not acting like a daft, flirty fool:

1. **Don't use femininity as a cop-out.** Don't fake frailty where frailty doesn't exist. Don't claim biology when biology isn't a factor. Don't manipulate people. Don't play dumb.

2. **Know thyself**—and set yourself up for success accordingly. If you know that you get a little sensitive or emotional for a few days each month, be aware of that. There is absolutely no shame in it—zero—but make sure that you give your body the rest, nutrition, and breathing room it needs.

3. **Don't assume sexism.** If you are passed over for a promotion or someone does you the kindness of offering to help, don't assume sexism. Not every knock is discrimination. Just ask yourself how you can be better, and go kill it. Don't operate with a chip on your shoulder; it's not becoming.

4. **Accept help.** Strong girls know it's wise to accept help. When I urge girls not to play helpless or coy, I'm not talking

about accepting help or chivalry; I am The Queen of Accepting Chivalry. Open my door? Yes, please. Take my car to get it detailed? Thank you very much. Pay for my dinner? I'll have the Ahi tuna steak—*and* dessert. I'll also take your coat because I'm chilly, and I want to be the first off of a sinking ship. Accepting chivalry and help doesn't demean or take advantage of guys; manipulation does, and therein lies a world of difference. In fact, accepting chivalry builds guys up. I make no bones about the fact that my husband has come to my rescue a thousand times in a thousand ways. I love him, I need him, and I feel safe when he takes care of me. There is no weakness in that; there is love in that.

I'm not talking about accepting help, either. I need people to help me with the heavy lifting, literally and figuratively. Life is hard, and we are in it together. We carry each other through and sometimes we carry each other's couches and refrigerators and boxes of books. If you don't accept help when you really need it, you're going to end up looking like a twit anyway because you're going to fail—or drop a box of books on your head. Accept help; it makes you humble and gracious; it makes you human, and a friend.

5. **Work hard.** Be creative. Take risks. Keep learning. Teach yourself to set goals that make people raise their eyebrows and say, "Wow!"

6. **Build appropriate relationships.** Relationships matter; networking is not the same thing as manipulating. Allies are different from flirting pawns. All movement in life is about who you know and how well they like you. Reputation matters. (This

is why you don't want your reputation to be that of a twit.) Be a friend, find a mentor, be a mentor.

7. **Be confident.** Assume you can. Do things that scare you.

8. **Don't lose your femininity.** You are a woman, don't lose sight of that! Femininity is a superpower. We don't need androgynous leaders, we need chick leaders. Use your feminine strengths; plan for your feminine weaknesses. Be unashamedly, uninhibitedly womanly.

9. **Be your truest self.** If you love something, dare to really love it—unapologetically and without disclaimers, in a totally nerdy way. Author John Green wrote, "Nerds like us are allowed to be unironically enthusiastic about stuff. Nerds are allowed to love stuff—like jump-up-and-down-in-your-chair-can't-control-yourself love it. When people call people nerds, mostly what they're saying is, 'You like stuff,' which is not a great insult at all. Like, 'You are too enthusiastic about the miracle of human consciousness.'" Amy Poehler says it this way, "When you are interested in something, your life becomes more interesting and you become more interesting. Caring is cool." Be you without reservation. If you feel strongly about something, stick to your guns. If you believe in something, advocate for it. Fill the void that only you can fill by being the person only you can be—you. I'll tell you the same thing I told my daughter on school picture day when we were practicing smiles at the breakfast table: "Let your insides sparkle out."

So do yourself a favor; don't act like a space cadet or a Barbie or a coy, giggly, flirty idiot to get what you want. Ask for it. Work for it. Go get it. Be real; be yourself.

Sparkle.

THINK IT THROUGH, TALK IT OUT

1. How does a girl act if she is "playing princess"?

2. List some reasons that playing "princess" is hurtful to girls and to women.

3. Why should you, as a teenager, care about the "long-term effects" on the way women are perceived?

4. Of the "ways not to act like a twit" at the end of this chapter, which is the most difficult? Which is the most inspiring? Which one do you think you're the best at? Which one will you decide to work on this week?

"Always be a first-rate version of yourself instead of a second-rate version of somebody else." –Judy Garland

"Be yourself. Everyone else is already taken." –Oscar Wilde

"Let me know that You hear me Let me know Your touch. Let me know that You love me And let that be enough." –Switchfoot

I studied advertising in college. I paid a good sum of imaginary loan money (which I will be repaying with *real, actual* money until the day I die or until the rapture, whichever comes first[23]), for a mass communications degree with a double specialization in advertising and public relations. I worked in marketing for exactly three months before I moved states, found out I was pregnant, and stayed home to raise my babies. If the point of college had been the degree, it would have been a colossal waste of time and money. Good thing the point wasn't the degree; it was the education. I've used the education every day since. I've used it in my marriage, my ministry, my parenting, and my writing. Plus I met my husband in college, so I'll go to my grave insisting it was worth every penny, DAD.

What I know about advertising is that one of the primary objectives is to create need. In order for you to buy something, you have to believe that you *need* it. You need it because it's useful, because it will save you

---

23. FREE TIP: IMAGINARY LOAN MONEY IS NOT ACTUALLY IMAGINARY. IT IS REAL, ACTUAL MONEY. So is credit card money.

time or effort. You need it because it's convenient, or a sign of wealth and popularity. You need it because it will make you happy, or pretty. You need it because it is cuter than all the other book bags or purses or pairs of boots. You need it to wear to school, or to the movies. You need it because it's delicious, or healthy. You need it so that the boy in your fourth period class will notice. You need it because you want it, or because you're worth it. You need it because it's on sale, because you'll never find it this cheap again. Every ad, every slogan, every campaign is designed to make you feel like you *need this thing*—over the absence of it and over every other product or brand.

Another thing I know is that any product with a television commercial isn't a necessity. There are no commercials for bread, bananas, school uniforms, or tap water. You never see a commercial for a modest, one-bedroom home. The commercial is for a real estate agency, and it features stately, upper-middle class homes and a Realtor driving a Benz. You need a home; they create need for the "American Dream."

There are no commercials for basic soap. The commercials are for body washes and shaving gels that smell like raspberry rain and are guaranteed to nourish forty-seven layers of skin and also get you a tall, fit, well-dressed, hygienic, football player for a boyfriend while it's at it. You need soap; they create need for "sensual" soap.

If you really need a thing, there's no point in advertising because you're going to buy it anyway. It's like what Tina Fey says about unsolicited mom advice, "No one ever says, 'You really must deliver the baby during labor.' If you really must do a thing, it doesn't need to be said." Companies know that the only way to get your parents to buy the upper-middle class home and get you to buy the get-a-boyfriend body wash is to make you believe that you *need* it.

I recently saw a Crest commercial wherein a very hot (and well-dressed) guy with fabulous hair sees his ex-girlfriend and does a double take because she's laughing with a huge, ear-to-ear, Rachel McAdams kind of smile and her teeth are so white. Then he walks over and starts flirting with her because her teeth are so white. Crest is implying that the hot guy regrets breaking up with his girlfriend BECAUSE HER TEETH ARE SO WHITE.

In what kind of weird alternate universe is this a plausible scenario? First of all, no girl would be that friendly to a guy that dumped her. If you like it then you shoulda put a ring on it, man. And did this guy break up with this girl because her teeth weren't white enough? Are the teeth a metaphor for her personality? That's the only thing I can figure, because I'm pretty sure I could whiten all the livelong day and none of my exes are going to come banging on the door to grovel.

Axe products are another terrible offender. The slogan for their shampoo is "Get some hair action," and it is accompanied by scantily clad women (in their mid-twenties) getting aroused while running their fingers through a pimply, middle school boy's greasy hair. Talk about a suspended reality. Middle school boy hair is disgusting. Congratulations, Axe, that is Creating Need—Level Expert. You know every boy that watches their commercial is all, "MOM, I NEED THIS SHAMPOO. NO, YOU DON'T UNDERSTAND. I **NEED** IT."

To create need: this is the agenda of every ad in existence.

You won't get the job without this breath mint.

You won't get the hair without this shampoo.

You won't get the status without this car.

You won't get the guy without this teeth-whitening cream.

This agenda is what makes the beauty industry so dangerous. Think this through with me: in order for a beauty company to create need where need does not exist, they must make you dissatisfied with the way things are now—with the way *you are* now.

The ugly truth about advertising is that your self-image is collateral damage—an unfortunate, but acceptable, consequence in the bigger picture of industry growth. Hear me: the beauty industry is not the enemy. The people in the advertising industry don't hate girls, and they are not out to decimate your self-esteem. In fact, many of them are working hard to empower you and all the other girls in your generation. But the fact remains: every single day you're alive, you are exposed to hundreds of messages intentionally designed to make you unhappy with yourself.

If that weren't sad enough, think about the frequency of the You Need To Be Better messages. You are surrounded by marketing every minute of every day; you're drowning in it and you don't even know. On your phone, on the games you play, online, at school, in every store window and on every rack of clothing, on television, in movies, and in magazines. Did you know that marketing companies pay people to get on Facebook and Twitter and Instagram and Tumblr and whatever else and talk about how much they like their products? That people are *paid* to like and share and blog about stuff? Every minute of every day you are receiving messages that say, "You need improving; your as-is self is not enough." It is a bombardment, an onslaught.

> every minute of every day you are receiving messages that say, "you need improving; your as—is self is not enough."

Your universe implies:

You are not thin enough. Your skin is not tan enough, or light enough, depending on your ethnicity. What we're really saying is that your skin is not latte-colored and racially nondescript, like someone who is Latin or Middle Eastern. But heaven forbid you look discernibly Latin or Middle

Eastern, because that's no good either. Your teeth are not white enough or straight enough. Also, your breath will never be fresh enough.

Your skin is not young, firm, smooth, tight, hydrated, or pore-less enough. You don't look airbrushed enough. (Um, does anybody?)

Your legs are not long enough, and your thighs touch. (There is a huge collective of women whose biggest concern about their bodies is that their *thighs touch*.) Your legs are not smooth enough, and while we're at it, neither are your armpits. (Does anyone else think it unreasonable that prickle on a woman's legs is such a scarlet letter? My prickle happens in like an hour and a half. I used to spend forty minutes just shaving my legs, bringing my total shower time to AN HOUR because I thought if I pressed hard enough, was thorough enough, my legs would stay smoother longer. It took me years to make peace with the fact that I am not made of synthetic plastic; I am human—made of flesh and blood and HAIR and I should stop wasting my time in the shower despairing over rate of return on my leg hair. Whatever, man, I shaved. I did my part. That's all anyone can ask of me.)

You are not tall enough. You are too tall. You don't have enough curves. You are pear shaped; we have Spanx for that.

Your toes are too long and your heels are too rough. Your lips are not pouty enough, or shiny enough, or outlined enough. Your eyelashes are not long, dark, thick, or curvy enough. (Do our eyelashes really need to be ALL those things? Those are very high expectations for the hairs that grow out of our eyelids.)

Your stomach is not flat enough. Your rear end is not curvy enough. Your breasts are not big enough, or perky enough. (Never mind that it defies the laws of physics to have breasts that are both large AND perky.)

Your nails are not strong enough. Your hands are not soft enough. Your hair is not long enough, shiny enough, silky enough, straight enough, curly enough, thick enough, or voluminous enough. You are not stylish enough, modern enough, hipster enough, classy enough, popular enough, or wealthy enough.

Then these companies say, "Here, let us help. We can fix you."

Except, no. They can't.

These messages program you for dissatisfaction at best, and at worst, they program you to really, sincerely believe that you are so flawed and undesirable that you are unworthy of romance, friendship, respect, or love. It is the great mercy of God that any of us are even remotely well-adjusted.

In this sense, it is every girl against the world. It is you looking up into the face of a looming tsunami—standing in its shadow. It is all the dollars in all the pockets of all the executives versus you. How could anyone survive that? How will you?

From my childhood and into my twenties, I suffered from uncharacteristically high self-esteem. I was jealous of other girls because everyone is jealous of other girls, but mostly I believed that I had it going on. My body image took a small dip after my first and second babies, and went into an all-out tailspin after my third, but even now I find shades, whispers, of my high self-esteem of yore. When I go shopping, for example, I pick a pair of shorts that I *know* will fit. But when I get to the dressing room, I literally cannot get them over my thighs. Unfortunately, that is not an exaggeration. I actually believe myself to be three sizes smaller than I actually am, no matter how many pairs of pants tell me otherwise. I guess I just give myself the benefit of the doubt; my default setting is to believe that my clothes are fitting well, my hair is falling fabulously, and my skin is looking great. I believe this so unswervingly that I am often jarred by my own reflection. I catch a glimpse of myself and think, Wait, what? This thing must be distorted, because I look way better than this chick staring back at me. All mirrors and cameras are liars; I believe that.

Because of my better-than-average body image (and without much introspection), I assumed that I never struggled with insecurity—that I had somehow been spared the constant striving and measuring up that tortured so many of my peers.

This illusion came crashing down one night during my senior year of college. That whole year, I lived with a vague, overarching sense of desperation. It was like a fine mist of anxiety that touched both everything and nothing. Everything was fine, except it wasn't. On the second night of my spring break I sat on my bed at home—reading and journaling. I was reflecting on my relationships,

> it was like a fine mist of anxiety that touched both everything and nothing. everything was fine, except it wasn't.

and considering my spiritual and emotional state when these words materialized on my page, in my own handwriting:

"I just want someone to <u>enjoy</u> taking care of me. I want to be worth it."

The word "enjoy" is underlined, and the whole page is smattered with tear drops.

I stared at the words for a moment. Then, it was as if the levies that had been holding back the cumulative fears of twenty-one years burst. For the first time, I felt what had been there all along, nagging from just below the surface of my consciousness. "I am a burden. No one will ever really know me because no one will ever want to press on as long as it takes to know me."

The inadequacy was crushing; it knocked the wind out of me. The fear was acute, piercing. I felt the striving fully, agonizingly. I recognized entire facets of my personality as the behaviors of a girl trying to squeeze herself into everything a young woman should be: confident, friendly, a good conversationalist. Independent, not needy; only a joy, never a burden. Cute, flirtatious, beautiful, intelligent, and demure.

My insecurities were (and are) more social than physical: I need too much, I feel too much, I am too quiet, I am too shy, it is hard to know me, I am not worth the trouble it takes, I am not enough.

I felt as if my heart had curled up into the fetal position, tiny, tight, and cramping. I sat there on my childhood bed, looking and feeling very much like a little girl, and I wept. I said to

my insecurities were (and are) more social than physical: i need too much, i feel too much, i am too quiet, i am too shy, it is hard to know me.

God, "You take care of me; You know me; You enjoy taking care of me" over and over, until I almost believed it.

Those same tired insecurities are still hanging around, but I recognize them now, so they don't knock the wind out of me anymore. As an adult, what I want more than anything is for someone to tell me, at the end of every wearisome day, "You've done enough."

I've learned that the "not enough" message isn't exclusive to you or to teen girls or to women whose bodies bear the marks of birthing three children. It isn't even specific to body image, and it is no respecter of persons. The most beautiful, self-assured, powerful, productive woman longs to hear, at the end of every long day, "You did enough. It is okay to breathe now. You are enough." The girl at your school with perfect skin and a perfect nose and great hair and the best figure and all the clothes you could never afford longs—aches—to hear, "You are enough."

THE SCALES

Imagine a scale; on one side are all the messages of affirmation and sufficiency you receive in a week: a daily "I love you" from your mom, a church service, a girl-power Lady Gaga or Katy Perry song on the radio. On the other side of the scale, imagine the messages of insufficiency you receive in a week: a gushing fire-hydrant of ads designed to create need, an onslaught of images of girls that have been Photoshopped within an inch of their lives. The high school caste system, and social media likes and follows—a cruelly measurable indicator of popularity.

The imbalance is staggering. It makes me angry. It makes me sad—to think of all the girls who are tortured by self-hatred every time they dress, undress, shop, shower, or pass a mirror. It makes me feel compassion; I see so many of the dumb things you all do (silly clothes, bad flirting, drama, eating disorders, cutting) as your very best (and sometimes most desperate) effort to reconcile what you are with what you feel you need to be. It makes me desperate for my daughter to know that she is beautiful—that she is valuable, and enough. And it motivates me; we must fix the imbalance—right this ship.

The solution to the imbalance isn't balance. If a scale is tipped and you add equal measure to both sides, it stays tipped. The solution to imbalance is *counterbalance*. I can't just tell you you're beautiful and get on with it. Your mom can't just tell you you're enough and expect that to carry you through the tsunami you're going to have to walk through. You can't just compliment your girlfriends and expect that to make a dent. We don't just tell each other we're enough. We wage war.

We . . . wage . . . war!

IMBALANCE   BALANCE   IMBALANCE

IMBALANCE   COUNTERBALANCE   BALANCE

The message we take to the front lines is, "You are enough." It is the epitaph on our banners, the crest on our shields, our battle hymn.

This radical message of sufficiency, of intrinsic value and worth, is the only truth that carries enough weight to tip the scales of self-worth. No attack on the beauty industry will make you respect your body. Flattery and clichés are lightweights. We could pile a thousand "You are beautiful to me's" and "It doesn't matter what anyone else thinks about you's" and "You're perfect just the way you are's" onto the scale and it wouldn't amount to a heap of feathers.

The reason "You're perfect just the way you are" isn't reassuring is because it's not true—and we know it. The reason it doesn't make us feel better is because we know better. We know too much of our own flaws and broken places to be persuaded that we're perfect just the way we are, no matter how enthusiastically anyone insists. Platitudes don't heal hearts; truth does.

> Just maybe, if someone tells us often enough, if someone loves us steadfastly enough, we could dare to believe that we are enough.

We are tired, short-tempered, pimpled, anxious, selfish, envious, insecure, gossipy, frizzy-haired, prickly-legged creatures. We can never believe ourselves perfect—but maybe, just maybe, if someone tells us often enough, if someone loves us steadfastly enough, we could dare to believe that we are enough.

You don't need better self-esteem. Self-esteem is empty and baseless and arbitrary. You can't just decide you're awesome for no reason and expect that to give you the courage and conviction you need to go through life. You don't need to believe you're awesome; you need to know—really know—that you are enough.

> You are enough because God declares you so; this is the great scandal of the gospel.

You are enough because God declares you so; this is the great scandal of the gospel.

God invented justice. He hates evil more than you, in your moral superiority and human self-righteousness, could dream. He banished Lucifer to hell for his blasphemous pride. God knows that the price of sin is death, and He requires the shedding of blood for the forgiveness of sins. He is utterly holy, perfectly pure.

You lie and cheat and steal. I do too; that's what we get for being people. We are filthy, tainted by our prejudices and our selfishness. We are ungrateful, lustful, lazy, and idolatrous. With our minutes, hours, and dollars we idolize our friends, grades, families, comforts—even our own bodies. Imperfect is a weak euphemism; we are abhorrent.

A just God and a sin-sick people have no business engaging in a great love affair, but we are. Tim Keller wrote, "You are more sinful than you could dare imagine, and you are more loved and accepted than you could ever dare hope." The gospel is scandalous. God doesn't love you because you are enough—you are enough because He loves you. You are enough to be loved radically. You are enough to be pursued, ransomed, redeemed, bought back, sacrificed for, rejoiced in, cleansed, purified—worked on and in and through. You are not perfect, but He is perfecting you.

> GOD DOESN'T LOVE YOU BECAUSE YOU ARE ENOUGH—YOU ARE ENOUGH BECAUSE HE LOVES YOU.

INTERNAL

God doesn't look at the things people look at. People look at the outward appearance, but the Lord looks at the heart (see 1 Samuel 16:7). If God knows the exact number of hairs on my head right now (which my hairdresser tells me is astronomical), He must see my prickly legs too. But the jet-black prickles on my porcelain-white legs are not a factor in my worth; they are completely irrelevant to my enoughness, thank God. God is only concerned with the temporary as it relates to the eternal. He cares about my body as it pertains to my health, my self-discipline, my modesty, and my self-worth. The rest is neutral. He cares about the way your room is decorated only to the degree that it reflects your spiritual condition: if you spent money you shouldn't have spent, that matters. If you have things hanging on the walls that can't glorify Him, that matters. If you use it to entertain, welcome, help, and serve, that matters. If you use it to hide and hoard, that matters. Beyond that, it's neutral, so don't worry too much about it. God is only ever concerned with what matters; He never needs a perspective shift. He IS the big picture. He IS wisdom. He IS the truth. And the thing that God cares about, the thing He looks at, is hearts.

God cares not one iota about my prickles or the bags under my eyes. He is concerned with whether I pursued Him or my coffee more zealously this morning.

There is this incredible story in the New Testament where some guys bring Jesus a man that is paralyzed and lying on a mat. Jesus rewards their faith by telling the man, "Your sins are forgiven"—because He knows that the man's biggest problem isn't his legs; it is his heart. Of course, everyone around thinks Jesus is (1) blasphemous, (2) crazy, and (3) a little bit of a punk for not healing the guy, if He can in fact heal people. And get this:

> Knowing their thoughts, Jesus said, "Why do you entertain evil thoughts in your hearts? Which is easier: to say, 'Your sins are forgiven,' or to say, 'Get up and walk'? But so that you may know that the Son of Man has authority on earth to forgive sins. . . ." Then he said to the paralytic, "Get up, take your mat and go home." And the man got up and went home. When the crowd saw this, they were filled with awe; and they praised God, who had given such authority to men. (Matthew 9:4–8)

Jesus did a physical miracle to demonstrate His authority, to get us to consider: which is more difficult to deal with—paralysis or sin? Which matters more—legs or soul? The obvious answer is souls—hearts. This is what matters to God. Nobody had to die for God to heal paralytics, but someone had to pay in blood for the sins of the world; perfect justice requires it. The redemption of our souls is why Jesus came; all the healing was just to get our attention.

And so, if God, in His omniscience and holy zeal, sees all my ugliness of heart and still declares me enough, why should I ever despair? If He can handle my sin, how much more can He handle my baby weight? God tells us that physical training is of some value, but godliness has value for all things, holding promise for both the present life and the life to come (see 1 Timothy 4:8). He tells us that our beauty should not come from outward adornment, such as elaborate hairstyles and the wearing of gold jewelry or fine clothes. Rather, it should be that of your inner self, the unfading beauty of a gentle and quiet spirit, which is of great worth in God's sight (see 1 Peter 3:3–4). Anne Lamott says, "Joy is the best makeup." I know people like this, people who glow—and one of my highest ambitions in life is to become one. I want to have a beautiful spirit, to be gentle, to be described as kind.

It is your heart that matters, and your heart is loved. It is your soul that endures, and your soul can be redeemed. The externals are neutral—temporary and fading fast (see Proverbs 31:30). The internals are where your value lies, and your internals are enough.

ETERNAL

You are enough to matter eternally. All the days ordained for you were written in His book before one of them came to be (see Psalm 139:16). When God breathed life into Adam's lungs, it was already written that you

> GOD DECLARED YOUR WORTH AT CREATION AND AFFIRMED IT ON THE CROSS, LEAVING NO ROOM FOR DOUBT.

should live. Your eternal past existed in His mind and heart; you mattered. When you entered the world in your broken, sinful, body, the plan to rescue you was already in place—already in play: Jesus would pay the ransom for your soul. Your eternal future existed in His mind and heart; you mattered. God declared your worth at creation and affirmed it on the cross, leaving no room for doubt—you are doubly valuable: made and redeemed. Doubly loved: breathed and bought.

You are enough internally and eternally. You are enough, doubly, in every way that matters.

If your mother resented you, you are enough. If your father left you, you are enough. If your boyfriend cheated on you, you are enough. If you have an addiction, you are enough. If you are depressed, you are enough.

You aren't perfect, or awesome, or the best. This isn't about just-for-the-fun-of-it self-esteem. But you are enough in every way that matters.

> NO GROVELING OR CONFESSION OR MAKING AMENDS REQUIRED. YOU ARE ENOUGH TO BE LOVED, RIGHT NOW.

Right now, in this freeze-frame. No tweaks, no change of clothes, no slapping on mascara or sucking in your belly or rubbing lotion over scaly parts. No groveling or confession or making amends required. You are enough to be loved, right now.

The end of *Good Will Hunting* is one of my favorite scenes in any movie that's ever been made: there is this amazing scene where abused, hardened, hurting Matt Damon collapses into his therapist's arms and sobs, while his therapist (played by Robin Williams) says over and over, "It's not your fault. It's not your fault. It's not your fault." The emotion is thick—tangible. I weep for relief with him every time. Deep breath. Catharsis. It's not your fault.

I suspect that if a therapist were to take any given girl by the shoulders, if he were to look deep into her eyes and insist, "You are enough. You are enough. You are enough," she would collapse into his arms and weep. I suspect that her knees would give way, unable to stand up under the relief of it. I suspect that all of us would be undone as we, battered and bruised, climbed out from under the weight of all of the things we've been measuring ourselves against for our entire lives.

"You are enough." This is the truth with which we wage war on insecurity. This is how you fight for your moms and sisters and friends and selves: you tell them as many times as it takes for them to hear it. And I will go all Robin Williams on you; I'll unleash the deluge. I will speak it, shout it, whisper it, sing it, write it. You put it on your mirrors and doors and refrigerators; you put it in your cars and lockers and inside of your binders (see Deuteronomy 6:6–8). You memorize it, and I will too, and I'll pray it over you and me and my daughter and all of us. You and me and your mom and your grandma and your youth leader and your teachers and your coaches and your neighbors and the girls at school, even the ones you hate: we'll blast each other and we'll allow ourselves to be blasted. We'll say it over and over until we dare to believe it. "You are enough."

This truth—the scandalous love of God that calls us beautiful and valuable and enough—will rescue us all over again.

You need it. Shy girls, scared girls, loud girls, attention-addicted girls, girls who date recklessly, rebellious girls, religious girls, girls who cut, girls who eat and girls who don't, girls who cry in bathroom stalls: you need it.

Women need it. Moms who spend, plan, fret, flirt, binge and purge, clean, and volunteer like they have something to prove need it.

Guys need it. Guys that lift, guys that deck out their trucks with lift kits, guys who are scared almost the whole way to death to talk to a girl—guys who are striving to measure up to some unattainable standard of stoic masculinity need it. They are enough too.

Kids that don't quite fit into the spaces that the world has carved out for them—kids that communicate or learn or whose bodies work a little differently—need to know it.

People who are hurting, hiding, aching, and searching need to know it: you are enough. No more striving; there is nothing left to earn (see Ephesians 2:8–9). You are accepted—loved.

We all need it; we need it to survive our march through the gauntlet—and it is a gauntlet. I know because I've lived it. I *am* living it. I've been living in a female body in this world for twenty-eight years, and the weight of thousands of not-enough beauty messages caught up with me on the eve of my twenty-seventh birthday, when I should have been rejoicing in my third baby, and instead I was despairing over how thick my arms were. "I was enough when I was the skinny one, but I'm not enough now." That's the lie I'm waging war on today. I'm having to practice what I preach—desperately, religiously coming to Jesus and letting Him remind me, "You are not perfect; I am perfecting you. You are loved, internally and eternally. You are enough."

If you let "enough" trickle down from your ears—down, down, down—and let it seep deep into the soil of your heart, it will change your life.

You will grow in humility, because you'll stop trying to convince yourself and everybody else how perfect your life is.

You will fall more and more in love with Jesus—because His grace and kindness and love will amaze you. You'll know how secretly screwed up you are, how much of a total crazy person you are—and when you think about how much, and how faithfully, unrelentingly, and powerfully Jesus loves you anyway, it will blow you away.

You'll be free to dress how you want, to create your look without trying to get attention from any girl or boy or parent—because you're enough. You won't have to ruin your skin in a tanning bed because you're enough the way you are RIGHT NOW. You won't have to smoke, play dumb, or flirt your way into what you want. You won't need to date idiots, wilt under the pressure of your course load, wear a size 2, or have five hundred followers on Instagram.

What you need is Jesus.

When the guy you can't stop thinking about doesn't know you exist, you can come to Jesus and be assured, "You're enough."

When your dream college (or your safety college) says no, you can come to Jesus and remember "You're enough."

When you mess up in an irreversible way, when there are consequences, you can come to Jesus and hear, "You're enough."

When an advertisement asks, "Is your skin too dry/oily/pimply/uneven/blotchy?" You can dare to say, "No." You can dare to believe that you don't need every fix for every thing that is purportedly wrong with you.

If you want smoother hair, fine, but as you fire up the flat iron, remember: you're enough. If you want to drop 10 or 20 or 85 pounds, great. But with every step, every overhead press, every lunge remember, "I'm enough." With every pound shed, "I'm enough." With every binge, "I'm enough." Every pound gained back. "I'm enough." Your value is not contingent upon your success in any area. Not one. Not goodness, not honesty, not skinny-ness or popularity. You have value because you are a person. You have value because God says you do. This is God's story; His love makes you enough.

Don't spend your whole life aching and yearning and measuring up because it will kill you. Come to Jesus and let Him save you, redeem and perfect you. Come drink deeply of His grace. Come to Jesus and let Him tell you, "You are loved, darling. You matter, darling. I am enough for you; you are enough for Me. Believe and rest."

Be still.

Be quiet.

Breathe. Just breathe for a minute.

You are loved.

You are enough.

THINK IT THROUGH, TALK IT OUT

1. Kate mentioned a toothpaste commercial that was designed to make girls feel like their ex-boyfriends would be jealous and regretful if their teeth were whiter. Think about the commercials on TV now—what things are they trying to make you believe that you need? If you think about them long enough, do they start to sound ridiculous? What is the silliest one you can think of?

2. Why do ads designed to create need make us feel like nothing about us is "enough"?

3. What does Kate mean when she says that you are "doubly enough"? What is the first way God established your value? How did He insist on your value a second time? Why is this special?

4. What is the difference between self-esteem and confidence? What does the Bible say about self-esteem? What does the Bible say about confidence? How do humility and confidence go hand-in-hand?

5. Is "enough" enough? Why do we want so badly to be perfect?

6. Kate talked about waging war against insecurity and the message of "not enough." How can you wage war for yourself (your own mind)? How can you wage war for your friends? How can you wage war for all girls?

7. Kate said that she knows women who glow with peace and joy and wisdom and kindness. Do you know women who seem to glow with an intangible kind of inner beauty? Who are they?

APPENDIX

10 THINGS I WANT TO TELL TEENAGE GIRLS
MARCH 25, 2012

1. If you choose to wear shirts that show off your breasts, you will attract boys. To be more specific, you will attract the kind of boys that like to look down girls' shirts. If you want to date a guy who likes to look at other girls' breasts and chase skirts, then great job; keep it up. *If you don't* want to date a guy who ogles at the breasts of other women, then maybe you should stop offering your own breasts up for the ogling. You think you want attention, but you don't. You want respect. All attention is not equal.

2. Don't go to the tanning bed. You'll thank me when you go to your high school reunion and you look like you've been airbrushed and then Photoshopped compared to the tanning bed train wrecks formerly known as classmates—well, at least next to the ones that haven't died from skin cancer.

3. When you talk about your friends "anonymously" on Facebook, we know exactly who you're talking about. People are smarter than you think they are. Stop posting passive-aggressive statuses about the myriad ways your friends disappoint you.

4. Newsflash: the number of times you say "I hate drama" is a pretty good indicator of how much you love drama. Non-dramatic people don't feel the need to discuss all the drama they didn't start and aren't involved in.

5. "Follow your heart" is probably the worst advice ever.

6. Never let a man make you feel weak or inferior because you are an emotional being. Emotion is good; it is nothing to be ashamed of. Emotion makes us better—so long as it remains in its proper place: subject to truth and reason.

7. Smoking is not cool.

8. Stop saying things like, "I don't care what anyone thinks about me." First of all, that's not true. And second of all, if it is true, you need a perspective shift. Your reputation matters—greatly. You should care what people think of you.

9. Don't play coy or stupid or helpless to get attention. Don't pretend something is too heavy so that a boy will carry it for you. Don't play dumb to stroke someone's ego. Don't bat your eyelashes in exchange for attention and expect to be taken seriously, ever. You can't have it both ways. Either you show the world that you have a brain and passions and skills, or you don't. There are no damsels in distress managing corporations, running countries, or managing households. The minute you start batting eyelashes, eyelashes is all you've got.

10. You are beautiful. You are enough. The world we live in is twisted and broken, and for your entire life you will be subjected to all kinds of lies that tell you that you are not enough. You are not thin enough. You are not tan enough. You are not smooth, soft, shiny, firm, tight, fit, silky, blonde, hairless enough. Your teeth are not white enough. Your legs are not long enough. Your clothes are not stylish enough. You are not educated enough. You don't have enough experience. You are not creative enough.

There is a beauty industry, a fashion industry, a television industry, (and most unfortunately) a pornography industry: and all of these have unique ways of communicating to bright young women: you are not beautiful, smart, or valuable enough.

You must have the clarity and common sense to know that none of that is true. **None of it.**

You were created for a purpose, exactly so. You have innate value. You are loved more than you could ever comprehend; it is mind-boggling how much you are adored. There has never been, and there will never be another you. Therefore, you have unique thoughts to offer the world. They are only yours, and we all lose out if you are too fearful to share them.

You are beautiful. You are valuable. You are enough.

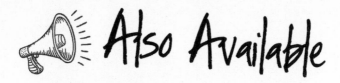

Also Available

ENOUGH

10 things
we should be telling
teenage girls

KATE CONNER

Chances are, if you're reading this, there is an "older" woman in your life (a mom, a sister, a mentor, a friend) who loves you and wants the very best for you. Invite her to read along in *Enough*, Kate's book for women based on her run-away blog post "Ten Things I Want to Tell Teenage Girls." Woven into each chapter is a powerful message of worth that transcends age, and will touch the souls of women, young and old alike: You are beautiful. You are valuable. You are enough.